Banff Natio

How Nature Carved

David M. Baird

Hurtig Publishers, Edmonton
in co-operation with
Parks Canada
and the
Geological Survey of Canada

Revised edition
Copyright © Minister of Supply and Services Canada 1977

Hurtig Publishers
10560 105 Street
Edmonton, Alberta

Co-published through
Publishing Centre
Supply and Services Canada
Catalogue No. R61-2/6-2

ISBN 0-88830-132-4 cloth
ISBN 0-88830-133-2 paper

Photographs: David M. Baird
Maps and diagrams: Geological Survey of Canada
Design: David Shaw & Associates Ltd.

Printed and bound in Canada
by T.H. Best Printing Company Limited

Contents

How to use this book

If you haven't the time immediately to read the general description at the beginning of the book, look at the illustrations and turn to the maps facing pages 64 and 208 to find out the numbers of the stops along the route you are travelling. Then turn to the roadlogs (starting on p. 81) and follow them carefully, for you will find that the beauty of the scene is greatly increased when you know more about what you are looking at, how it originated, and even the names of some of the principal features. Much more detailed maps than are possible in a book of this size are available at each of the park information centres and these make travel far more rewarding, for they show a great deal about the country you are going through.

The first part of this guidebook describes in some detail the general aspects of the geology and scenery of Banff National Park—exactly where it is, how the mountains there originated, what the rocks of the region are and where they came from, the different shapes of mountains related to the structures of the rocks composing them, and something about how the scenery came to be. This general background is followed by detailed descriptions of selected localities of special geological interest. The rest of the book comprises a series of notes on what is to be seen at each of the viewpoints and roadside stops along the main travel routes.

Most of the words used in a technical sense or which have an unusual meaning are italicized and are explained carefully where they are first used. If, however, you do not immediately find the meaning of a word, look in the index, for many of the unusual ones are listed there along with all place names and a great variety of subjects.

Although all measurements are given in metric units, the imperial equivalents have been added where it is felt they will be helpful. All distances between roadside stops are given in miles as well as kilometres.

Besides benefiting from the information in this book it is hoped you may discover, peeking out here and there, some of that feeling of awe and wonder which springs in the breasts of all people who visit the beautiful mountain environment.

Introduction

Some of the most beautiful mountain scenery in the world is to be found in the Rockies of western Alberta and adjacent eastern British Columbia. An area of 6,641 square kilometres (2,564 square miles) in this region has been set aside as Banff National Park for the enjoyment of present and future generations of Canadians and visitors from other countries. Sharp jagged peaks and rounded mountains, slow-moving glaciers and dazzling white snowfields, rushing mountain streams and gentle rivers, narrow canyons and open wooded valleys, and alpine meadows and dense forests—all of these are preserved in their natural state.

The mountains and valleys in this part of North America trend northwest-southeast, and from high in the air appear as a series of parallel, serrate ridges and valleys. Next to the plains and foothills on the east, the mountains show strong *fold* and *fault* structures, having been bowed up in great arches and down into troughs, and are sliced by faults or fractures. Complicated rock structures are again to be seen along the western margins of the Rockies in British Columbia. In between, and making up a very large part of Banff National Park, are lines of mountains carved into horizontal and gently inclined layers of rocks which have been lifted high into the air. Here we find some very famous peaks, such as Mount Assiniboine and Mount Eisenhower.

In the rocks is written a long and complicated history of ancient events, beginning with the spread of seas over the land half a billion years ago. Where rocks are exposed along road-cuts, in valley bottoms and on the peaks, we can see how thousands of metres of sand, silt, and gravel were deposited in the shallow marine waters by rivers, and along the ancient shorelines by waves, and even far from

5

shore by ocean currents. In the ancient seas that covered what is now an area of snow-capped mountains, marine creatures lived and died. Their remains, in the form of imprints or actual shells and other hard parts, are now found as fossils in the rocks that came from these sediments millions of years later.

High in the mountains, great icefields still cover large areas and send down tongues of glacial ice into adjacent valleys. Meltwaters from the icefields and last winter's snow form rushing streams and beautiful waterfalls. In some places where stream valleys have been dammed by glacial debris, lakes are formed, with some taking on a glorious turquoise or pale green colour from glacial silts in summer.

All through the mountains the processes of erosion may be seen at work, even now. The moving ice in the glaciers, the running water of streams and rivers, the wedging action of frost, the force of gusty winds, and masses of rocks and boulders slipping or crashing downhill, are all causing a steady wearing away of the mountains.

Thus, for the visitor who has time to stop and wonder a little about his surroundings, Banff National Park has a great array of magnificent scenery and numerous features of geological interest in the rocks into which the scenery is carved. The person interested in the beauty of what lies before him will find it even more moving when he reflects on the intricately woven patterns of events that down through millions of years have produced the rocks and the mountains, the rivers and the glaciers. It is the purpose of this book to tell you something of all these things—the beauty, the formation of the scenery, and the history written in the rocks—and at the same time to share a little of that reverence that comes to those who know nature well.

Boundaries of the Park

The entire western boundary of Banff National Park, from its southernmost point at Palliser Pass, to the Snow Dome, 160 kilometres to the northeast, is the Continental Divide, which there also forms the boundary between Alberta and British Columbia. In a straight line the distance is about 160 kilometres, but following the serpentine, twisting boundary itself the distance is close to 320 kilometres. From the Snow Dome in the northwest, the boundary curves westward in a great horseshoe, with the open side to the north, along *divides* that separate northwest-flowing waters and ice of the Sunwapta river system from streams flowing southeast into the headwaters of the North Saskatchewan River. It is this boundary that crosses the main Banff-Jasper highway at Sunwapta Pass.

From the northeastern corner of this horseshoe-shaped bend—the northernmost point in Banff National Park—the boundary extends for about 40 kilometres southeasterly along the divide between waters flowing southwesterly into the North Saskatchewan River and those flowing more easterly onto the plains. There it crosses the North Saskatchewan River, and about 8 kilometres farther on it turns abruptly from its generally southeasterly course, parallel to the mountain system, to a northeasterly course that takes it out onto the plains. From the crossing of the North Saskatchewan River, the park boundary continues along a series of minor divides in a general southeasterly direction to near Conical Peak, where it swings easterly across the Siffleur River and thence northeasterly along minor divides for another 24 kilometres. From this point, about 8 kilometres northwest of the Clearwater River, the boundary follows a series of local divides between tributaries as it crosses the Clearwater River, the Red Deer River, the Panther River, and the Dormer River, and thence southward to Mount Aylmer about 64 kilometres away. From this peak, visible from the Banff area, a looping bulge on the eastern side of Banff National Park takes in Lake Minnewanka and the area drained by tributary streams. Surveyed lines then take the boundary across the main Trans-Canada Highway (the eastern park entrance) and up the side of Mount Rundle to its

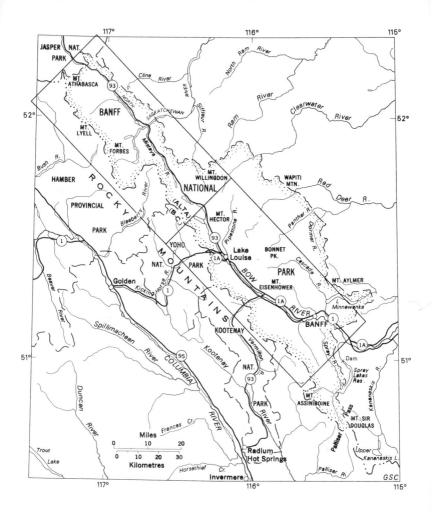

Banff National Park, showing area covered by roadlog maps.

8

uppermost edge. This it follows to the southeast to the end of the ridge. From there the boundary is a series of surveyed lines up the valleys and the crest of ridges southwestward around Spray Reservoir and on to the southernmost tip of the park again.

As a quick summary, it may be said that Banff National Park encloses an area on the eastern slope of the Rocky Mountains from the Continental Divide, including the drainage area of the Bow River above the village of Banff, the headwaters of some easterly flowing streams to the northeast and southwest, and the drainage area of the North Saskatchewan River and its tributaries above its junction with Owen Creek, about 5 kilometres downstream from where the Banff-Jasper highway crosses the river.

Divides

Even the largest rivers rise in a multitude of very small streams, which make up the bulk of the main river by uniting their waters. All of them gradually get smaller as you go upstream beyond the tributaries that pour water into them from the sides. If you travel farther and farther up a stream, you will eventually come to where it begins as a tiny trickle of water. Such a place is usually near the top of a hill, for as rain falls on the hill it will naturally flow down the slopes on all sides. Thus, the crest of a ridge forms a natural divide between waters that flow down one side and waters that flow down the other. This is why, on the ground or on a map, a line drawn to separate two drainage systems is called a *divide.*

A look at a map of North America will quickly show you that some very large rivers flow into each of the oceans bordering this continent. If you were to follow these rivers to their very headwaters, you could establish a line separating the drainage to the Pacific Ocean from the drainage to the Atlantic Ocean, and other lines that divide Atlantic drainage from Arctic drainage and Arctic drainage from Pacific drainage. Thus, the imaginary lines that separate the major drainage areas of a continent are called *continental divides.*

Ever since man first began to separate territories, it has been convenient to divide them on the basis of drainage basins of rivers. Boundaries of countries, provinces, or even counties have commonly been defined as the divide between the water flowing to one side and water flowing to another. One such boundary is between the Province of Alberta and the Province of British Columbia. This divide, which runs right up the spine of the Rocky Mountains, separates waters that eventually end up in the rivers to the Pacific Ocean from those that will flow finally into the Atlantic Ocean. It is this same Continental Divide that forms the twisting western boundary of Banff National Park for 320 kilometres. This means that a cup of tea spilled at any point on the part of the boundary made by the Continental Divide would flow half to one side of the line and half to the other, and would eventually reach two different oceans. In fact, there is one spot in North America where drainage is split among three oceans, and at this spot—on the crest of the Snow Dome in the icefields where Banff and Jasper national parks come together—your spilled cup of tea would flow eventually into the Arctic Ocean, the Atlantic Ocean, and the Pacific Ocean.

Shapes of Mountains

Travellers in the mountains have long noted the distinctive shapes of individual mountains. Coming into Banff National Park from the east you see the skyline of the high Rockies beyond the foothills, with tall sharp peaks, more gently rounded ones, and others with one side steep and the opposite one more gently sloping. Entering Banff from the north, the west, or the south through the mountainous country, you notice the great variety of the shapes of the mountains.

Distinctive shapes of individual peaks are due to a combination of three things: the kinds of rocks in the mountain, the structure of the rocks within the mountain, and the particular tools or agents of erosion that have carved the mountains. In Banff National Park the rocks into which the mountains are carved are of *sedimentary* origin, that is, they were once fine muds and silts, sands, and gravels that lay in the bottom of shallow seas. Over the millions of years after their

Mount Eisenhower is an outstanding example of a castellated mountain.

deposition, these sedimentary materials became *sedimentary rocks* and are now sandstones, shales, and limestones.

Long after they were made into solid rocks, the flat-lying original layers were subjected to enormous stresses within the earth's crust so that they were folded and broken along fractures called *faults.* Thus the mass of rocks into which were cut the Rocky Mountains in Banff National Park present a wide assortment of rock types, which now vary from flat-lying to vertical and from parallel-layered to crumpled and *folded.* Add to this a variation in the tools of erosion, principally glaciers and rivers, and you can see how the many different shapes of mountains are formed. The hundreds of peaks and mountain masses, however, belong to only a few kinds—the ones described below and shown in the photos.

Castellate, Castle, or Layer-cake Mountains

Mountains that are cut into more or less flat-lying sedimentary rocks commonly have profiles in which vertical steps alternate with flat or sloping terraces. Some such mountains look very much like ancient castles and are thus said to be *castellate* or castle mountains. Mountains of this kind are best developed in regions underlain by great thicknesses of rocks in which *beds* or layers of massive limestone and sandstone or quartzite alternate with less resistant beds of shale or slate. The softer rocks are eroded more rapidly so that the harder rocks are undermined and tend to break off at right angles, forming steep slopes and cliffs. Steep-sided needles and pinnacles are sometimes left on the tops of such mountains as the uppermost massive layers are cut away. The best example of this kind of mountain in all of our national parks is probably Mount Eisenhower which, until it was renamed after World War II, was actually known as Castle Mountain. Pilot Mountain is another superb example in Banff Park.

Mountains Cut in Dipping Layered Rocks

Some mountain peaks are cut into masses of layered sedimentary rocks, which *dip* or slope from nearly horizontal to 50 or 60 degrees. Some of these have one smooth slope that follows the dip of a particular rock layer from its peak almost to its base and, on the other side, a less regular slope, which breaks across the upturned edges of the layered rock units. Mount Rundle near the town of Banff is a good example and, when reflected in the calm waters of the Vermilion Lakes, provides one of the very beautiful views in the Canadian Rockies. Other mountains, like Mount Edith Cavell in Jasper National Park, are cut into dipping sedimentary rocks in such a way that neither side follows the dipping rock layers and thus both sides are irregular.

Dogtooth Mountains

Sharp, jagged mountains sometimes result from the erosion of masses of vertical or nearly vertical rocks. The peaks may be centred on a bed of particularly resistant rock, in which case a tall spine or rock wall may result. Mount Louis and adjacent peaks on the west side of Forty Mile Creek north of Banff are spectacular examples.

Dogtooth mountains result from the erosion of vertical or nearly vertical rocks.

Below: A light dusting of snow tops Rundle's crest with white. Its reflection in the still waters of the lake presents yet another variation in the almost infinite series of beautiful views of this mountain.

Above: Sawtooth mountains, like those seen here in the Sawback Range, are formed when steeply dipping sedimentary strata are eroded by cross gullies. *Below:* In this steep-walled valley, sixteen kilometres north of Banff, the rocks have been folded into a very tight anticline, or upfold, and pushed right over.

Other peaks like those in the photo on page 13 are found in the Amiskwi area of Yoho National Park.

Sawtooth Mountains

If the rocks in a long ridge are vertical, or nearly vertical, erosion may produce rows of angular mountains that look like the teeth in a saw. This type is superbly shown in the Sawback Range from Mount Ishbel southward to where the Bow River swings across the mountains near Banff. The same kind of mountains is well shown again in the Colin Range east of Jasper.

Irregular Mountains

Many mountains are cut into more or less homogeneous masses of rock and, as a result, have no particularly characteristic shapes. These we may call *irregular mountains,* although individual peaks may be round, conical, pyramidal, or shapeless, depending on how they were cut. Many of the mountains in the eastern and northeastern parts of Banff National Park would fit here.

Anticlinal Mountains

In some regions of folded rocks, mountains are underlain by great up-bowed or arched masses of rock. Such upfolds are *anticlines* and the mountains are called *anticlinal mountains.* Stretching of the rocks on the outside or upper layers results in numerous fractures which in turn make the rocks more susceptible to erosion, so that true anticlinal mountains are rare. Several anticlinal mountains, not individually named, are to be found in the Fairholme Range northeast of Banff.

Synclinal Mountains

Mountains are commonly cut into masses of rocks that have been folded into great arches and troughs. Erosion over a long period may cut away all the surrounding rocks to leave a mountain with a trough

15

or bowl structure within it. This probably comes about because the folded rocks in the centre of the trough, called a *syncline,* are more resistant to erosion than those in the surrounding parts, which tend to split and break during folding. Cirrus Mountain near the north end of Banff National Park and Mount Kerkeslin in Jasper National Park are examples. Mount Eisenhower is also a synclinal mountain, although its internal structure is not readily visible from the main highway.

Mountains of Complex Structure

Anticlines and synclines, that is upfolds and downfolds, may be seen in the flanks of some mountains that have been developed on tightly folded rocks. These we may call *complex mountains* because of the complex structures of the rocks within them. Magnificent examples can be seen all along the eastern edge of Banff and Jasper parks.

Matterhorn Mountains

When glaciers cut deeply into rocks that are more or less homogeneous, they carve bowl-shaped depressions called *cirques.* When several cirques are cut into a mountain mass but are stopped by a warming of the climate and consequent melting, they sometimes leave sharp semi-pyramidal towers of rock to which the general term *matterhorn* is given. Mount Assiniboine near the southern end of Banff National Park is an outstanding example in the Canadian Rockies.

Shapes of Valleys

Valleys are different, too, in their shapes and their relationships to the rocks underneath them. The great gash in the earth which forms the Grand Canyon of the Colorado River is markedly different from the broad, open valley of the lower Mississippi. Similarly, in Banff National Park, the narrow canyon filled with the rushing waters of

At the southeastern end of Lake Minnewanka this peak shows complex structures.

Below: The great synclinal or troughlike structure of Cirrus Mountain can be seen clearly here.

The mighty peak of Mount Assiniboine soars 3,618 metres (11,870 feet) above sea level. In this view over Lake Magog, from just outside the park boundary in British Columbia, one can see why this mountain is called Canada's Matterhorn.

Johnston Creek is very different from the flat-floored valley of the Bow River nearby. These differences reflect the age or relative stages of development of river valleys.

When mountains or plateaus are first uplifted by the enormous forces within the earth's crust, rivers and streams that develop on them tend to be fast flowing and to cut down into the rocks very rapidly. In this way they form canyons and steep-walled valleys that are termed *youthful valleys*. When rivers have had a long period of geological time to cut their valleys, they eventually wear them down to a level where the river slows. Other forces of erosion will cut down the valley walls and gradually widen the valley so that it becomes more open. After a very long period of stability, the country surrounding the river may also be cut down so that the valley itself becomes a broad flat-bottomed one with very gently sloping sides. Such valleys ultimately become *old age valleys*. The present Rocky Mountains, in which Banff National Park is situated, have been uplifted in fairly recent geological times so that all the streams in the area are either youthful or just barely mature. Something that has complicated their histories very greatly, however, is the geologically recent period of glaciation. This was a time of lower temperatures in which snow and ice accumulated to a much greater extent than now, filling most of the valleys and covering most of the peaks. When the glaciers melted back to their present positions, great quantities of rock debris, from boulders to the finest of rock flour, were dumped into the river valleys.

Another way to consider valleys is in their relationship to the rock structures underneath them.

Anticlinal Valleys

In regions of folded rocks, stretching in the outside or upper layers in anticlines, or upfolds, may result in numerous fractures, which in turn make the rocks more susceptible to erosion than those of adjacent areas. Thus streams often carve valleys along the crests of anticlines, and such valleys are called *anticlinal valleys*. For many kilometres, the Banff-Jasper highway follows the crest region of a very large and long anticline which you can see clearly in the anticlinal dips or slopes near Bow Peak.

Synclinal Valleys

Valleys are commonly located along the troughs of synclines or downfolds. This is sometimes directly related to the folding process, but in other cases the history of valley-cutting is much more complex. From the main Banff-Jasper highway in the region of the big hill south of Sunwapta Pass, you can see that the rocks on each side of the valley dip in toward the road in the valley bottom.

Fault Valleys and Others

In mountainous regions where rocks have been severely folded, they often break; and along these great fractures one mass of rocks may be moved past another. Such a line of breakage would be particularly susceptible to erosion and thus some valleys are placed along faults in the earth, being called *fault valleys*. Another reason for valleys to erode along faults is the way in which movements sometimes place a group of very soft, easily eroded rocks against a resistant rock member. The valley produced in these circumstances could also be called a fault valley. Fault valleys are very common along the eastern side of Banff National Park.

Still another way to classify valleys is on the basis of the particular tools of erosion that have left the most profound imprints on them. A river valley, for example, is one that has been carved by a river. It may be shaped like an open *V* in cross section, with the river filling the whole of the valley bottom, or it may be much more open with a flat bottom and flaring sides. When tongues of ice occupy a valley, they tend to cut into its sides so that when the ice melts away it leaves a valley that is flat bottomed and has nearly vertical walls. The resultant shape corresponds more or less to the letter *U,* and such valleys are said to be *U*-shaped.

Thus you see, from even a preliminary glance at the mountains and valleys in a region like Banff National Park, that the scenery is the result of various processes of erosion working on masses of rock, and that differences in these things will make differences in the kind of scenery you look at. When you see the differences from place to place in the patterns of trees and flowers, and in the animals and birds that depend on them, you come to realize that all of the natural scene ultimately depends on the long geological history that lies behind the mountains and the valleys.

Origin of the Mountains

Banff National Park is a mountain park so that any understanding of its scenery requires a knowledge of how mountains originate.

Any survey of the surface of the earth soon shows that there are mountains of many different kinds. Some stand as isolated masses whereas others occur in groups that are clearly related to one another. Some tower thousands of metres above their surroundings whereas others may be only a hundred metres high, even though they are called "mountains" by the people who live there. The wide variety of mountains points to a wide variety of origins.

In some parts of the world, great masses of liquid lava and ash pour up from the depths of the earth to accumulate around volcanoes. These form *volcanic mountains.* In other places, rivers and streams have cut deeply into high plateau areas over long periods of time to leave rough mountainous terrain. In still other parts of the world, huge wrinklings in the earth's crust are made by tremendous compressive forces, in the same way that you can wrinkle the carpet on a floor by pushing against it with your foot. Thus *folded mountains* are made. Another type of mountain results in places where the earth seems to have split along enormous faults or breaks and one of the sides is uplifted one or two thousand metres. These are *fault-block mountains.*

When, however, we come to the great ranges of mountains—groups of clearly related mountains that extend for hundreds or even thousands of kilometres over the surface of the earth—we find a much more complicated story. One of the most interesting parts of

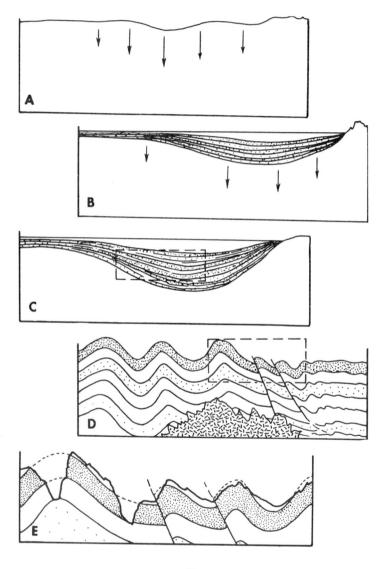

Development of Geosynclinal Mountains

The spectacular peaks and valleys of the Rocky Mountains as we know them today are made of rocks which record a story that began more than 600 million years ago. At that time part of western North America began to warp downward to form an elongated trough as in A.

Rivers poured sand, silt, and gravel into the lowland area. Downwarping continued until the trough was filled with a shallow sea, into which poured a steady flow of sedimentary materials, as in B.

Downsinking continued, but it seems to have been at a rate that corresponded closely to the rate of filling, so that sedimentation was always into shallow marine waters. The mass of sedimentary materials slowly changed to sedimentary rock as the load on top increased until it had a form like that in C.

For reasons we do not yet understand, the trough area was then severely compressed so that the rocks in it were folded and broken. At about this time in the history of such mountains great masses of molten materials commonly appear in the cores of the folded and broken rock, eventually solidifying into granite. D is what an enlarged section of C would look like.

Uplift accompanied the folding and faulting, and as soon as the rocks emerged from the sea they were subjected to erosion. Rivers and glaciers carved the valleys and formed the peaks as shown in E, an enlarged part of D. This is the stage of development of our Rocky Mountains now.

this story is that the major mountain systems all over the world seem to have the same kind of history, with at least several chapters in common. We call this type *geosynclinal mountains,* and it will help to know something about how they originate, for the mountains in the western Canadian national parks are of this kind.

To begin the story of Canada's western mountains, we must go back into geological time at least 750 million years or even 1,000 million years. North America then was very different from the land we know today. Where we now find the Rocky Mountain System from the Arctic Ocean to Mexico, there existed a great flat area that was very close to sea level. Great forces in the interior of the earth, not really understood yet, caused the whole area to sink very slowly. The rate of this depression was probably only a few centimetres in a thousand years, but it continued over a very long period of time. Ultimately it resulted in the flooding by the sea of hundreds of thousands of square kilometres of what we look upon now as the interior of North America. Into this vast shallow inland sea, the rivers from the surrounding regions poured their loads of silt and mud, which spread evenly over the bottom. Waves eroded the shores of these ancient seas, added more sediments, and made currents to distribute them over the bottom, far from land.

As the millions of years passed, the accumulation of sedimentary materials—the mud, silt, and sand from the rivers and shorelines, and limy *precipitates* from the sea itself—gradually filled the shallow inland sea. At times, when vast areas must have become filled to near sea level, one would expect that these processes would stop. But one of the strange things about these great depressions in the earth's surface is the way they seem to have continued to sink as the load of sedimentary materials in their centres increased. By this gradual sinking and an almost equal rate of filling, it was possible for thousands of metres of sand, silt, and mud to accumulate, layer upon layer, and show features of shallow-water origin throughout.

During all of this time, living things were undoubtedly present on the surface of the earth, but we have very little record of them. At a time in the earth's history which geologists place at between 600 million and 500 million years ago, living things began to populate some parts of the seas fairly thickly. Some of these creatures had hard skeletons or outer coverings, and when they died these hard parts fell to the bottom and were promptly buried by the accumulating muds and silts. In some places the hard parts of the dead animals made clear impressions on the sedimentary materials on the sea bottom. When the soft sedimentary materials hardened into solid rocks, perhaps over periods of millions of years, the remains and imprints of the long-dead organisms were preserved in them as fossils.

How do we know these things took place where we now find the western mountains? The answer is to be found in the rocks themselves where the story is fairly clearly written but must be deciphered by geologists, the historians of the earth's past.

The rocks of which the mountains are made are clearly of sedimentary origin—that is, they are made of ancient gravels, sands, muds, and various sediments that have become hardened into solid rock. They are layered or *stratified* as we would expect accumulating sediments to be, because from time to time there were changes in the composition of the material being laid down and the ways in which they were laid down. These changes may have been due to storms, changes in wave patterns, changes in drainage systems, or the changes that would take place as the land supplying the sediment was gradually being eroded away. On some of the rock surfaces we can find ripple marks that are exactly like those found today in stream bottoms or in the shallow parts of the sea. Some of the rock surfaces are dimpled with impressions of raindrops and mud cracks as though they had been exposed at low water. Impressions of salt crystals on some rock beds suggest that drying went on for a long time. By splitting open the rocks, we can find the fossilized remains or the imprints of ancient sea creatures, some of them with modern counterparts. Other fossilized skeletons are from creatures that have been extinct for millions of years, but we can tell a great deal about them by comparing their structures with those of present creatures that are somewhat similar, and by noting carefully their association with creatures we know something about.

The kinds of materials the rocks are made of and all the structures found in them can be observed today in different parts of the world in the actual process of formation. We can estimate the extent of the ancient seas by looking for the rocks that were deposited in them. We can tell something of the existence of former shorelines by looking for evidence of beach deposits in the rocks. We can tell whether rocks were laid down as sediments in deep water or in shallow water by comparing what we find in the rocks with what we see being deposited in those environments now. We can tell that at times the sea withdrew temporarily from a region or that the sediments completely filled the shallow depression on top of the continent. In short, by putting together and correlating hundreds of small pieces of scattered evidence, we can unravel with some certainty the story of the rocks from which the mountains were later carved.

A second stage in the history of the Rocky Mountains seems to have begun about 200 million years ago. The rock record tells us that a disturbance of the very shallow depression on the surface of western North America, which, as we have observed above, was filling with sedimentary materials, began to change the pattern of development. Some areas of the old trough were lifted up out of the sea and were themselves eroded to supply sediments that were poured back into the remaining sea.

As the tens of millions of years passed, the crust of the earth apparently became more and more unstable in the region of what we now call the Rocky Mountains. This unrest culminated about 75 million years ago in a complete change. The great thickness of rocks that had been accumulating as sediments on the old sea bottom in the previous billion years was lifted above sea level, broken in many places along great *faults,* and, in some places, strongly compressed. The compression or squeezing caused the great blanket of rocks to fold and buckle and, in places, to break so that one part slid over another. The forces within the earth that caused this kind of uplift and breaking are so vast that it is difficult to comprehend them at all. Yet we can go to the mountains and once again see clear proof of this chapter in the development of the Rocky Mountain System.

In very old mountain systems of the world, where long-continued erosion has cut into the very core of the mountains themselves, we can observe in some detail a third stage in the development of geo-

26

synclinal mountains. It seems that during or just after the folding and faulting, great masses of hot molten rock appear in the cores of mountain systems. These push rocks aside or melt their way into the interiors of the belts of folded and broken sedimentary rocks, where they cool slowly and eventually solidify. Canada's Rocky Mountains have not been deeply enough eroded for us to know anything about this part of their history.

The next phase in the development of all geosynclinal mountain systems seems to be one of quiet stability, during which the agents of erosion—glaciers, rivers, and wind—contrive to cut deeply into the uplifted, complicated mass of broken and folded rocks. Every now and again the erosional story is complicated by additional uplift. For some 70 million years now this has been the history of the Rocky Mountains in Canada.

At the present time, as we drive through the river valleys and among the mountain peaks, we can observe this stage of erosion as it proceeds. We can actually watch the glaciers pushing and scraping over the country, tearing off rock and grinding it up, some of it as fine as flour. We can see the rivers cutting into their rocky courses, wearing away the land, and carrying their loads of waste towards the ocean. We can observe great masses of gravel, sand, and silt—the result of erosion of mighty mountains through tens of thousands of years—now spread out below the foot of the mountains. And we can see where erosion has cut valleys deep into the complicated rock structures to reveal much of the story of folding, faulting and uplift.

For a very long time, scientists wondered why mountains occur where they do and why this kind of a history has taken place where it has. Now, within the decade of the sixties and the early seventies, a realization that the outer sections of the earth behave like enormous plates moving about on a mobile substrate, has suddenly made possible an understanding of many of the puzzles concerning the origin of major features of the earth's structure.

From a variety of lines of evidence, it is clear now that inner parts of the earth are plastic under the enormous pressures and elevated temperatures prevailing there. It seems, too, that currents moving infinitely slowly are generated in this plastic layer by the earth's inner heat sources. We all know that the outside of the earth, the part we run around on, is solid; and it is conceived that sections of the outer solid part are moved about by the drag of the currents on their undersides. Thus, like ice cakes in a river in spring, enormous sectors of the earth's solid layer move against one another, bumping and scraping, and riding over and under one another on a scale that deals with whole continents and ocean basins in size, and with a time scale that takes millions upon millions of years to move a few hundreds of metres.

The real cause of mountains lies in this motion of the earth's great plates. Take a look at the Rockies, and you will realize that the whole of North America is being thrust westward against a great block of the earth's crust under the floor of the Pacific Ocean, and merely wrinkling up the edges a little. All the rest follows from this grand concept.

The Sculpturing of the Mountains

As soon as rocks are exposed they are subjected to the ever-present erosive action of rain, running water, falling snow, moving ice, frost, and chemical decay. Our western mountains have been exposed to this erosion now for many tens of millions of years. Running water has been by far the most important of all the agents of erosion in the carving of the mountains as we know them now. For millions of years streams have carried away the debris of all the other forces of decay and erosion, and have themselves carved valleys deep into the landscape.

Erosion may begin on the tip of the highest peak where the freezing of a thin film of water under a boulder may wedge it out and tumble it over the edge of a cliff. Heavy rains may loosen bits of rocks and boulders or may lubricate others so that they too join the downward rush. Thus, fragments of rocks are torn from the solid mountains and begin a long journey toward the sea.

Their first resting place may be in one of the long fan-shaped accumulations of angular blocks and pieces of rock which we can see

28

on the sides of every steep mountain. These are called *talus* or *scree* slopes, and their steepness is generally the maximum angle at which the loose rubble is stable. Climbing on them may be very difficult, particularly on the lower parts, which consist of very large, angular boulders and chunks of rock, lying in all attitudes where they have rolled or fallen. This means that not only will the surface of the talus or scree slope be very rough and irregular, but the slightest disturbance—even the weight of a passing man—may cause more sliding and adjustment of the blocks and particles in it. Rain may wash the rocks on the talus slopes and remove very fine particles and rock flour.

Rivers washing directly against the bottoms of the talus slopes may carry off some of the boulders and rubble, so that angular pieces

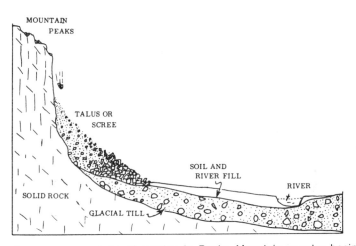

A common sequence of erosion in Rocky Mountain country begins when boulders and smaller particles of rock are wedged off the bare rocky peaks and fall to the talus or scree slopes below. Physical and chemical breakdown of the rocks in the talus produces fine-grained materials which move in the wash of rain and in streams, towards the river. A layer of glacial till made of a mixture of boulders, sand and clay commonly blankets the solid rock underneath the soil and river-fill in such valleys. In many places the glacial till is actively eroded by the river and thus contributes directly to the load of sediments on its way to the distant sea.

This scree cone extends into the waters of Moraine Lake.

and fragments now become part of the mass of boulders, gravel, and sand in the bottoms of stream valleys. Constant rubbing of boulders and pebbles against one another gradually wears them down, and the fragments that are worn off become very finely divided rock flour that looks like mud or silt in the water of a stream. Over the ages, the mass of rocks in the mountains is gradually worn away by the forces of erosion and carried ultimately to the sea, where it rests on the bottom as mud, silt, or sand. These materials may be the beginnings of new rocks and, in time, even new mountains.

In regions where mountains are being folded and faulted, broken and uplifted, various agents of erosion, notably the streams, may carve a whole set of valleys and mountains at one stage of development only to have their work completely changed by further uplift, movement along the surfaces of faults, and new folding of the rocks. Another cycle of erosion may reshape or completely modify the outlines of the mountains and valleys of the previous cycle after renewed uplift.

Thus, in our Rocky Mountains, the great valleys and the main outlines of the mountains that we know now have been shaped by the action of running water in fairly recent geological times, after a long period of repeated upliftings and intervening periods of erosion. After this there came a period when most of northern North America was covered by a great ice sheet, rather like those on Antarctica and Greenland today. It is thought that this period of glaciation began about a million years ago and that it had at least four distinct stages when the ice spread widely over the northern part of this continent, separated by periods when most of it disappeared again. It seems likely that the last extensive glaciers retreated about 10,000 years ago and left the land almost as it is now. It has left its mark on the land almost everywhere we look.

Glacial erosion is of two kinds. When an area is covered by an ice sheet, more or less evenly, the movement of ice outward from the centre of accumulation tends to round off the bumps and smooth out the hollows. High in the mountains, however, the action of the glaciers is generally much more localized and accentuated. Around the margins of snowfields or icefields, glaciers push down the valleys, steepening them and deepening them as they go. In the areas of accumulation, great bowl-shaped depressions, called *cirques,* are sometimes carved deep into the mountain sides. These commonly have almost vertical back walls and rounded bottoms.

The cutting action caused by the movement of ice and snow toward the centres of cirques and the outlets of snowfields tends to steepen the scenery in the mountains and make it much more sharp and angular. Cirques that cut into two opposite sides of a mountain may leave a razor-sharp rock ridge where their two vertical back walls intersect one another. It sometimes happens that a round mountain peak of considerable elevation is cut into by cirques from several sides. If this action is interrupted by melting of the ice before the mountain is completely cut away, it may leave a semi-pyramidal tower of rock, like the world-famous Matterhorn in Europe, or Mount Assiniboine in the Canadian Rockies.

Long tongues of ice extending from snowfields down the valleys, as valley glaciers, commonly steepen the valley walls and push great

31

This hanging valley, with a white ribbon of falling water, is on the northwest side of the valley of Wolverine Creek. The falls are just visible in the distance from the Muleshoe Lake picnic site near the southern end of the old Route 1 A.

piles of rock rubble and debris ahead of them. The position of maximum penetration of such alpine or valley glaciers is commonly marked by great heaps of the debris they have left behind. Long *finger lakes* are sometimes found in valleys that were dammed up in this way, but in others the rivers were able to cut through the dams and drain the upper valleys.

Farther back, characteristic *U*-shapes were impressed on the valleys where their walls were much steepened and their bottoms were covered with blankets of glacial debris. Small streams, occupying shallow valleys on the shoulders of the main valleys, may now tumble over the edge in very high waterfalls. The high valleys that such streams run in are now called *hanging valleys.*

Thus, we can see how glaciers tend to sharpen the profiles of the mountains and the scenery. Bowl-shaped depressions with vertical walls (*cirques*), sharp ridges with nearly vertical sides, sharp angular mountain peaks, *U*-shaped and hanging valleys—all of these are characteristic of areas of upland glaciation.

Nowadays in Canada's western mountains we can see numerous glaciers and snowfields on the heights and in protected places. These are really remnants of the ice that once covered the whole area in the not very distant geological past.

In the few thousands of years since the glaciers modified the shapes of Canada's western mountains, rivers have resumed the carving and cutting of the great mass of uplifted rocks. Now, however, their valleys are choked with glacial debris brought from high places by the moving ice. In some places the cirques or bowl-shaped depressions carved by the glaciers are occupied by small lakes called *tarns,* and in other places the long valleys have filled with water behind dams of glacial debris to form long finger lakes.

Marks of the passing of the glaciers are visible everywhere in Banff National Park. Mountain peaks are characterized by cirques and glacially steepened walls. Beautiful lakes like Hector, Bow, Peyto, Mistaya, Louise, Moraine, and Minnewanka owe their beginnings to glacial scouring and damming of old valleys. The Bow River is busily distributing and redistributing a vast quantity of sand, gravel, and ground-up rock brought into its valley by the glaciers. Its course in the vicinity of Banff has been completely altered (see page 58). The drainage pattern has been modified in other places by dams and plugs of glacial debris so that waterfalls and newly carved canyons are a common part of the scene. Here and there, as on Wolverine Creek, beautiful waterfalls are produced at the ends of hanging valleys. Great quantities of water-washed sand and gravel from the melting glaciers blanketed the country in some spots and now form banks and cliffs where modern streams cut into them.

The Rocks

In the 6,641 square kilometres of Banff National Park only one outcropping of *igneous* rock—rock that at one time was molten—is known. All the other rocks were laid down as sediments in distant geological times in a succession of seas that covered what is now an area of mountains. As we found out when we investigated the origin of the western mountains, these sediments eventually solidified to form solid rocks that were later thrust up into their present structures. In order to appreciate the scenery and to understand why certain mountains and valleys are where they are, and are the shape and colour they are, we should find out something about these rocks— what kind they are, something of their origin and age and, for convenience of description, the way they are grouped into different units.

At the very beginning, we have to recognize that the whole rock sequence (and therefore the whole history in it) is not available in one place. The rock layers have been folded and faulted and pushed about so that to discover what the whole sequence of rocks looked like before it was broken, we must piece together fragments of the record from different areas. It would be very convenient indeed if we could find one place where a drill could penetrate the entire rock section from the very youngest rocks on the top to the very oldest ones deep below, or a steep-walled valley where everything would be exposed in one cliff. Geologists find early in their investigations, however, that their task is more difficult than this, what with the complex rock structures and the way that individual rock layers

34

thicken and thin and even pinch out altogether to be replaced by other rock units at the same horizon.

One other thing to consider about rock layers and the history and order of events in them is the *law of superposition*. Under ordinary circumstances, you would expect to find in any sequence of layered sedimentary rocks that the youngest rocks lie on top and the oldest ones below. The reason this would usually apply is to be found in the way these rocks originate — accumulating in layers of sand, silt, mud, and gravel, one after another on the bottom of the sea. When a road is built, a layer of coarse gravel may come first, followed by fine sand, then crushed stone, then coarse asphalt, with fine asphalt the last thing to be laid down on the top of the road. If we cut down through the road or bore a hole in it, we encounter the youngest layer in the top coat of asphalt and the oldest, the first layer put down, in the coarse gravel on the very bottom. So it is with the geological record. When we look at the layers of rock in the side of a mountain, the law of superposition will tell us that the oldest rocks are in the lowest parts and that younger rocks lie above them.

Study of the geology of western Alberta shows again and again that the great mass of sedimentary rock extending out under the plains area farther east in a more or less flat undisturbed sequence, has been severely folded and broken along *faults*. This was done by enormous compressive stresses somehow related to fundamental forces deep within the framework of the earth. Compression has even gone further than folding and breaking the rocks, for we can see abundant evidence that the great masses of rocks have been pushed for long distances up and over other masses of folded and broken rocks so that in some places older rocks actually lie on top of younger ones. This structural complication does two things to make the order of rocks a little unusual. In some places the law of superposition does not work because older rocks lie on top of younger ones; and, secondly, rocks that we might normally expect to occur only deep below the surface are now found high on the mountain peaks. Then again, to find out what lay above some of the ancient rocks in the original sedimentary layered sequence, we have to travel out to the plains and drill into the topmost layers there.

Here, in the mountains a few
kilometres east of Banff, rock layers
are clearly folded into a great
downfold or syncline that extends
from the face of the ridge opposite
back into the mountains beyond.
Recent wastage from the steep cliffs
accumulates at the bottom as talus or
scree slopes.

Thus, the sorting out of the original sequence of rocks in all the mountain parks of western Canada has been a complicated problem for the geologists who have worked there.

In any area the rock sequence can usually be divided into units of various types in terms of thickness and areal extent. It is the custom of geologists to give names to recognizable rock units, and such names generally indicate places where the rock units were first discovered and described or where they are best exposed. Where there are masses of layered rocks, geologists use different names to indicate the different layers and groups of layers. An individual layer may be called *bed* or *stratum;* thus we might refer to a *limestone bed,* a *limestone layer* or a *limestone stratum.* A group of such beds, layers, or strata that has some distinctive characteristic in common is called a *formation.* An example in Banff National Park is the *Banff Formation,* consisting of a hundred metres of thick, brown-weathering limestone and shale layers. The Banff Formation is always found between two thick limestone formations, the *Palliser Formation* below and the *Rundle Formation* above. These three formations are found in many of the conspicuous peaks in Banff National Park, such as Mount Rundle and Cirrus Mountain.

Precambrian rocks: The table on page 39 shows in graphic form what the entire rock section in Banff National Park would look like if you could see it in one place with the youngest rocks on top and the oldest rocks on the bottom. You may note that the oldest rocks shown belong to the *Precambrian* period of geological time, that is they are older than 600 million years. In Banff National Park these are mostly grey, slaty shales or *argillites* with a purplish, greenish or reddish cast on some of the surfaces. They started their long history as muds or sandy muds in the bottom of the ancient seas that covered this area and eventually they hardened into shales and argillites. During their long history they were squeezed and perhaps heated to a certain extent during mountain-building processes so that their mineral make-up was altered to include the development of fine, scaly mica. It is this mica that gives the rock the sheen that can be seen almost everywhere the rocks are exposed. You can see

AGE OF ROCKS	Surface	
Jurassic and (?) Cretaceous		Kootenay Formation (3000): Conglomerate, sandstone, shale, coal
Jurassic		Fernie Formation (1000): Sandstone, shale
Triassic		Spray River Formation (1000): Dark grey, red-brown siltstone, shale and dolomite
Pennsylvanian and (?) Permian		Rocky Mountain Formation (600): Limestone and dolomite, cherty and sandy beds, quartzite
Mississippian		Rundle Formation (1500 - 2000): Limestone and dolomite
		Banff Formation (1500): Limestone, argillaceous limestone and calcareous shale
		Exshaw Formation (75): Black limestone, black fissile shale
Devonian		Palliser (1000): Massive limestone and dolomite
		Fairholme Formation (1500): Dark grey and black, fine-grained dolomite
Ordovician		Mount Wilson Formation (410): White quartz sandstone
		Sarbach Formation (1120): Shale on bottom grading to thick-bedded limestone above
		Mons Formation (975): Limestone on bottom grading to shale on top
Cambrian Upper		Pika, Bosworth and Arctomys Formations (1250): Limestone, dolomite and shale
		Eldon Formation (1000): Dark grey to black dolomite, cliff-maker
Cambrian Middle		Stephen Formation (400): Limestone with interbedded shales
		Cathedral Formation (1000): Massive grey dolomite with sandy and shaly layers, cliff-maker; Mount Whyte Formation at bottom
Cambrian Lower		St. Piran Formation (500±): White and pink quartzite with some shaly beds; grades downward into exactly similar Precambrian beds
Precambrian		Divided by some into Jonas Creek Formation above and Hector Formation below, but many local names. Massive quartzite of great thickness above, cliff-makers; shaly and slaty shale beds below (totals several thousand feet thick)

Note: Numbers in parentheses refer to thicknesses in feet
Modified from A.S.P.G. (1955), page 149

G S C

Generalized geological section, Banff National Park

39

Moraine Lake reflects the highlights of the Ten Peaks and the fans of rock debris, some of which (on the left) extend into the waters of the lake itself.

examples of these ancient rocks in many places along the main roads in Banff National Park. Notable places are at the junction of Routes 1 and 1A, the junction of the main Trans-Canada and Banff-Jasper highways, and on the lower slopes of Mount Eisenhower, Storm Mountain, and (from a distance) all along the lower slopes of the Waputik Range. As a general rule these ancient slaty rocks weather to form gently rounded slopes, commonly covered by forests, contrasting with the rocks that lie next above them which more often form on sharp, angular topography and bare slopes.

Rocks laid down in the *Cambrian* period, that is, in the space of time from about 600 million years ago to about 450 million years

Sweeping curves are made by the layering in these slaty rocks at the junction of the Trans-Canada and Banff-Jasper highways just northwest of Lake Louise.

ago, consist chiefly of pinkish *quartzites* with some layers of green and purple slaty shales in the lower or older parts. These rocks started off as sands and here and there contain layers of pebbles. The rocks are very dense and hard, although fairly brittle. You can see them in road-cuts near the entry to Yoho National Park, in the cliffs and *scree* slopes on both sides of Lake Louise, at Moraine Lake, and in the pinkish lower slopes of the mountains along much of the upper Bow River valley, notably in Bow Peak, the Waputik Range, and Mount Chephren. These rocks are generally referred to as the *St. Piran Formation* for the greater part of their thickness, with the *Mount Whyte* being a thinner formation above.

Middle Cambrian rocks (about 530 million years old) are predominantly limestones and *dolomites* with interbedded shales. In many places the limestones and dolomites are very *massive* or thick and hard to split and they resist erosion, but the interbedded shales weather away easily so that the limestones and dolomites break off in great steep cliffs. Mount Eisenhower shows this to perfection in its great castlelike towers and minarets, with steep walls of Middle Cambrian limestone and dolomite separated by breaks made by the more gently weathering shales.

Upper Cambrian rocks: Rocks that formed sometime in the latest part of the Cambrian period of geological time, perhaps 500 million years ago, consist of grey limestones and dolomites, again of considerable thickness and often spectacularly exposed as along the sawtooth ridges of the Sawback Range. These rocks also may be seen capping Mount Amery and adjacent peaks. It is interesting to note that these rocks are probably the same age as those forming the mighty Rock Wall in Kootenay National Park and peaks like the Goodsirs and adjacent ones in Yoho National Park.

Cambrian rocks are unique in another way for they contain the first abundant fossils. Geologists have long conjectured on whether this is because life suddenly became abundant or whether life first changed to forms that might be preserved in the rocks. *Trilobites,* crustaceanlike animals, which have long intrigued man, are found beautifully preserved in Middle Cambrian shales in several parts of the mountain park area, with one of the finest localities in the world being found on the slopes of Mount Stephen in Yoho National Park.

Rocks of the *Ordovician* period, about 450 million years old, are next above those of Cambrian age without any real break, and because they are grey limestones and shales it is often difficult to distinguish the end of the Cambrian from the beginning of the Ordovician sequence. Ordovician rocks are generally found north of Bow Pass in Banff National Park, where they form most of the bulk of Mount Murchison and, across the valley, Mount Wilson. One of the formations of the Ordovician period, the *Sarbach Formation,* gets its name from Mount Sarbach in this neighbourhood.

A cap of dazzling white ice and a very large cirque in the near slope are special features of Mount Amery, which rises 3,329 metres (10,923 feet) above sea level.

An unusual formation of the Upper Ordovician epoch is the Mount Wilson quartzite, which can be seen from many places along the highway as it passes under the shadow of Mount Wilson. At Stop No. 81 in the Roadlogs you can look up and see the white quartzite, as much as 150 metres thick, capping the cliff tops. For a closer look at the rock itself you can collect pieces of it from the stream debris near the highway.

Rocks of the next youngest geological age, the *Silurian* period, are notably absent from Banff National Park and very little is known of what events went on in this area during that time, about 400 million years ago. On the other hand, *Devonian* and *Mississippian* rocks, approximately 350 million years old, make up the major part of the mountains east of the axis of the Bow and North Saskatchewan River valleys. The lower or earlier part of the Devonian period is represented in some places, notably the eastern parts of the park, by limestones, quartzites, *conglomerates,* and silty shales. The upper or more recent Devonian rocks consist of more than 600 metres of dolomite and limestone. The *Fairholme,* is the name given to a group of dolomites of many kinds, about 300 metres thick, with the *Alexo Formation* being sandy and silty dolomite at the top of this group. One of the great cliff-forming limestone dolomites in all the Rockies is the Upper Devonian aged *Palliser Formation,* which ranges from 200 to more than 300 metres thick. Overlying this is another 300-metre-thick rock unit, the *Banff Formation,* which consists of shaly limestones with silty and shaly beds interspersed through it. It in turn is overlain by another mighty limestone, the *Rundle Formation,* of Mississippian age, and as much as 600 metres thick. This tremendous Devonian-Mississippian rock sandwich, with the grey Palliser limestone below, the brownish weathering Banff shales in the middle, and the grey Rundle limestone above, forms many of the conspicuous and beautiful peaks in Banff National Park. Among these are Mount Rundle and Cascade Mountain near Banff itself, Cirrus Mountain in the northern part of the park, Pilot Mountain, Mount Inglismaldie and others near Lake Minnewanka.

The *Exshaw Formation,* only several metres thick, is black shale lying apparently between Devonian and Mississippian aged formations. This formation has long puzzled geologists as to its exact age and what it is doing there in the middle of a great limestone sequence.

In many of the limestones and shales of the Devonian and Mississippian formations in Banff National Park there are abundant fossils. Here and there, fossil reefs contain large quantities of corals and the shells and imprints of a great variety of creatures, many of them long since extinct. *Brachiopod* shells, something like modern clam shells but with a different animal organization, and washerlike fragments of stems and plates of *crinoids* are perhaps the most abundant of these fossils. Their numbers indicate that conditions in those ancient seas must have been ideal for bottom life; indeed, parts of the Rundle limestones and the Banff shales are made almost entirely of shells and fragments of shells.

It is the fossil reefs in the Devonian and Mississippian rocks un-

Mount Rundle's great Palliser-Banff-Rundle rock sandwich stands out clearly.

derneath the plains that provide the great oil and gas reservoirs of western Canada. Most of the oil fields seem to be directly related to the ancient coral reefs themselves, and some geologists believe that the origin of oil is to be found in the vast quantities of organic debris that accumulated at the bottom of the sea where animals lived and died in great numbers.

The *Pennsylvanian* and *Permian* periods, about 300 million and 250 million years ago respectively, are represented in some parts of the continent by extensive rock sequences, but in this part of North America the millions of years of these periods are reflected only by a thin sequence of rocks containing few fossils. They can be seen along the road above the dam at Lake Minnewanka, along the main highway west of the western Banff cloverleaf, and near Bow Falls. They consist of dolomite, sandy dolomite, sandstone, silt, and shale, and range from several metres to as much as 250 metres thick.

Most of the stone for the public buildings, gateways, and other structures in Banff National Park has been taken from this quarry on the east side of the Spray River, about three kilometres south of Banff. The rock is part of the Spray River Formation and it consists of steeply dipping layers of shale, argillite and sandstone, in some places rippled as in the right foreground.

The *Spray River Formation* of *Triassic* age, approximately 200 million years old, is widely known in the western parks because many of the buildings and gateways in Banff National Park and adjacent parks are built from rocks taken from this formation. The main quarry is in the Spray River valley a short distance above Bow Falls. The rocks are dark siltstones, shales, and sandy beds which break into natural flagstones. Large surfaces exposed in the quarry show many ripple marks and mud cracks, suggesting that the sediments that hardened to form these rocks accumulated in shallow water. These rocks may also be seen at Bow Falls, in the walls of the Banff Springs Hotel and many of the public buildings in Banff, in road-cuts along the Trans-Canada Highway west of the Vermilion Lakes viewpoint, east of the eastern Banff cloverleaf, and again in the area of Lake Minnewanka.

Jurassic and *Cretaceous* rocks, from the next most recent geological periods—between about 180 million and 70 million years ago—consist largely of shales with thin, silty and sandy layers here and there. In some places coal seams, representing partly distilled accumulations of plant debris, are found in Cretaceous rocks. At one time this coal was mined in the region just east of the eastern Banff cloverleaf where the towns of Anthracite and Bankhead were once located. Rocks of Jurassic and Cretaceous age are found only in the valley bottoms in the eastern section of the park, where they are preserved between the great ridges of older rocks that have been thrust up high on each side. Younger rocks of Upper Cretaceous age, known widely in the plains immediately adjacent to Banff National Park, are not found within the park boundaries except on the extreme eastern edges.

At the top of the geological column we find deposits of gravel, boulders, and sand, washed down from the eroding mountains in fairly recent geological time. These deposits were supplemented by great quantities of glacial debris representing the accumulation of waste brought down by the glaciers at a time when the whole area was very much more extensively covered by moving ice than it is now. At the very top of the column we have the sand and gravel washed down yesterday by the rains or in the rivers.

Regional Differences in the Mountains

Those who travel widely in the western mountains of Canada soon come to recognize a distinct zoning from east to west made visible by differences in the scenery, which in turn reflect differences in the underlying rock structure. East of the mountains, undisturbed flat-lying rocks underlie the plains from Manitoba to western Alberta. To the west the plains are succeeded by the *Foothills,* a region of folded and faulted rocks, which have not been greatly uplifted. The *Front Ranges* succeed the Foothills to the west again along a very sharply marked boundary line. It is this abrupt change from the Foothills to the Front Ranges that impresses the traveller so much as he comes in from Calgary or Edmonton over the gently rolling country and sees the line of mountains beyond. The Front Ranges of the Rocky Mountains are made of a series of *fault slices* of folded and broken rocks thrust together like overlapping shingles on a giant roof.

The region of the Front Ranges is separated fairly clearly from another zone of mountains to the west, called the *Main Ranges* of the Rocky Mountains. Here, the rocks at the surface are not as severely disturbed although they are faulted somewhat, uplifted, and deeply eroded. In this area are found many of the oldest rocks exposed in the whole Rocky Mountain System. Still farther west, the *Western Ranges* of the Rocky Mountain System are built along a belt of severe disturbance in which the rocks are much folded and broken.

In Banff National Park we find only the Front Ranges and the Main Ranges. The Foothills lie to the east of the park boundary and the Western Ranges lie beyond the western boundary in Kootenay and Yoho national parks in British Columbia.

The Front Ranges consist of a series of northwest-southeast-trending *fault blocks*—bodies of rock bounded by faults or fractures—of folded and broken rocks of Devonian to Cretaceous age. Each slice or block is composed of folded and faulted rocks and each mass has ridden up over younger rocks along westward-dipping or sloping surfaces. Erosion has cut deeply into the complicated pattern of rocks thus produced to make the present array of mountains and valleys. Resistant layers make peaks, and weak layers make valleys

48

and lowlands. In many places the valleys are underlain by younger rocks, with upthrust older rocks forming the mountains of each side.

This arrangement of *thrust blocks* is apparent to the visitor to Banff National Park along the main Trans-Canada Highway from well south of the park entrance to Mount Eisenhower in the Bow River valley. From the park entrance, the first several kilometres of the Trans-Canada Highway are along a major valley, here followed by the Bow River itself, located on Cretaceous rocks with the thrust-up peaks on each side being of much older (Devonian) limestone. As the road swings more westerly across the ends of the mountains, you can see very clearly how each range is separated from the one next to it by a large open valley. The *fault surfaces*—the surfaces along which dislocation has taken place—which separate the blocks on each side cannot be seen in very many places. Near the power station, however, the rocks underneath the fault surface are exposed and show considerable distortion. These visible rocks are *Mesozoic* in age, approximately 100 million to 200 million years old.

A great fault, called by some the *Castle Mountain Thrust,* runs the length of Jasper National Park and continues southward right through Banff Park. It separates the Front Ranges from the Main Ranges. The latter are characterized by a kind of mountain structure different from the Front Ranges and are therefore somewhat different in appearance. This great break or series of breaks enters Banff National Park in the valley of the Siffleur River and trends generally southeastward. It passes just east of Mount Eisenhower, then swings more southwesterly across the Bow River valley near Copper Mountain to continue southeasterly, passing near Mount Assiniboine and thence beyond the southernmost tip of Banff National Park. Not all geologists agree that this is all one fault surface nor do they agree on its exact location, but it seems apparent that the mountains on the east or southeast of this general line are different from those on the west or northwest.

The mountains of the Main Ranges on the westerly side of this enormous fracture in the crust of the earth include most of the famous peaks along the Continental Divide—from Mount Assiniboine, near the southern end of Banff National Park, through Mount

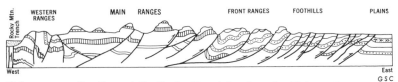

WESTERN
RANGES
Rocky Mtn.
Trench
MAIN   RANGES
FRONT RANGES
FOOTHILLS
PLAINS
West
East
GSC

This cross section through the Rocky Mountains, from the Plains to their western boundary, is greatly simplified to show the main features of their structural framework. In the east (the right in the diagram) flat-lying sedimentary rocks lie under the Plains layer upon layer, thousands of metres thick. In the Foothills the rocks are broken into steeply dipping slices, tilted so that each layer dips to the west, and uplifted so that rocks are brought from the depths up to or close to the surface.

The Front Ranges are made of slices of severely folded and faulted rocks which are uplifted and eroded so that layers that once were deep beneath the Plains are now at the surface, and in the valleys older rocks may be seen lying on top of younger rocks along each of the fault planes.

The simpler Main Ranges of the Rocky Mountains lie to the west of the complicated structures of the Front Ranges. They are cut into masses of sedimentary rocks which have not been severely folded but have been uplifted high into the air. Erosion has stripped off younger rocks, and today we can see the flat-lying older rocks high in the peaks.

The Western Ranges are cut into fractured and folded younger rocks. The western boundary of the Rocky Mountains is the Rocky Mountain Trench, indicated by the dotted pattern. It is filled with thick deposits of sands and gravels and is occupied by major rivers like the Kootenay, the Columbia and the Fraser.

Athabasca at the Banff-Jasper boundary, and on northwesterly to include Mount Edith Cavell and Mount Robson. All of these famous peaks have a similarity of appearance and the reason is they are all cut into uplifted and gently tilted sedimentary rocks.

The rocks of the Main Ranges are not severely folded but are thrown into open *anticlines,* or upfolds, and *synclines,* or downfolds, which trend generally parallel to the northwest-southeast grain of the country. A gentle syncline parallels the western side of the Castle Mountain Thrust from Mount Eisenhower (which used to be called Castle Mountain and from which the fault is named) northwestward to Mount Kerkeslin in Jasper National Park. All along this structure, the rocks dip gently southwestward into it from the northeast side and gently northeastward into it from the southwest side. In the very

The Banff-Jasper highway threads its way along the spectacular valley at the head of the North Saskatchewan River. At left is the nearly flat limestone peak of Cirrus Mountain at 3,216 metres (10,550 feet) in the centre of a great syncline.

centre the rocks are flat lying. This synclinal structure is clearly visible from several places along the Banff-Jasper highway, notably at the north end of Banff Park where, near the Big Hill, you can look northwestward and see Nigel Peak and southeasterly toward Cirrus Mountain. This synclinal structure is again visible from the vicinity of the crossing of the North Saskatchewan River, where you can see it in the end of Mount Wilson and the mountains to the east. The same structure may be seen in the southern end of Mount Eisenhower as you look at it from about 8 kilometres down the Bow River valley (see Stop No. 31 in Roadlogs, page 123).

The younger rocks occurring in Mount Wilcox and Nigel Peak (southern end of Jasper National Park) and Cirrus Mountain in Banff National Park occur where they do because the syncline, or downfold, sags in this area. This means that the older rocks on the sides plunge more deeply into the earth and the surface is made of younger rocks in the centre of the trough.

As you move away from the centre of this long syncline either eastward or westward, you come to the complementary anticline or upfold. To help visualize this structure, think of the shapes of the folds produced in a carpet when you push against it with your foot. The sides of downfolds or troughs are also the sides of the adjacent upfolds or arches. The anticline that parallels to the west the major syncline just described above may be seen in several places along the Banff-Jasper highway as, for example, in the area between Lake Louise Junction and Bow Lake. Here, the rocks clearly dip outward from the valley on each side so that the valley of the upper Bow River is clearly along the axis of the anticline itself. Bow Peak is made of nearly flat-lying beds or layers right on the centre of the anticline. In the northern end of Banff National Park the same general anticlinal structure is visible in the flat axial beds of Mount Amery and the peaks near the Big Hill. Thus, the scenery all along the Banff-Jasper highway depends pretty much on just where the road is in relation to the syncline and its paralleling anticline. The peaks and valleys of this area all have the same general appearance because the structure has a sameness to it. Individual variations depend on the accidents of erosion and the particular layers forming the peaks, contributing thus the characteristic shapes and colouring.

Areas of Special Geological Interest

Hot Springs

In 1883, surveyors for the Canadian Pacific Railway, then being put through the Rockies, noticed a cloud of steam rising from the lower part of what we now call Sulphur Mountain. When they went to investigate what it was, they discovered the first of many hot springs in the region of what is now Banff. Nowadays we know of several dozen places where hot and warm waters issue from the rocks here and there along the Rocky Mountains from the Hughes Range in the south to the Liard River in the Yukon. Many more undiscovered ones probably lie in remote valleys, in the bottoms of lakes, and in the bottoms of flowing streams.

At Banff, hot and warm springs are located on both the north and south sides of the Bow River valley. The largest and the best known are on the northeastern slope of Sulphur Mountain in a line nearly parallel to the ridge itself. The highest and hottest spring is Upper Hot Springs at an elevation of 1,584 metres (5,196 feet), issuing water with a temperature of 46°C (115°F). Its rate of flow varies somewhat but averages about 454 litres (100 gallons) per minute. The lowest of the springs are the Cave and Basin springs. The Cave Spring comes out of the rocks at the back of a sandy-floored cave at the east end of the swimming pool installations. The Basin Spring, at the other end of the pool installations, emerges at the foot of the cliffs and used to form a natural pool, but now is walled in. The flow of the Cave Spring is about 1,135 litres (250 gallons) per minute at a temperature of 29°C (85°F). The Basin Spring flows at about 681 litres (150 gallons) per minute at a temperature of 34°C (94°F).

In between these two areas lies the Middle Springs with a flow of 227 litres (50 gallons) per minute at a temperature of 33°C (92°F). A small subsidiary spring of the Upper Hot Springs (Kidney Springs) flows at about 91 litres (20 gallons) per minute at a temperature of 39°C (101°F). Across the valley a small spring, situated on the side of the old highway and known as Warm Spring, flows at about 227 litres (50 gallons) per minute at a temperature of 19°C (67°F). Another small spring is known as Forty Mile Creek, between Mount Norquay and Mount Brewster.

Each of these springs in its natural state consisted of an opening in the rocks from which water was issuing. Around the springs and below them, masses of spongy, brownish or pale yellow calcium carbonate is deposited in coatings or mounds. The material is precipitated from the spring water as it comes to the surface, cools, and evaporates. Noticeable in some of the road-cuts on the way up to the Upper Hot Springs are masses of this material from dead springs.

Careful analysis of the spring waters shows that the principal dissolved substances are calcium, bicarbonate, and sulphate, with a great deal of variation from spring to spring in the amounts of these substances in the water. Considerable carbon dioxide and small quantities of hydrogen sulphide gas are also dissolved in the water. It is the latter that gives the water of some of the springs the rotten egg smell. In addition to these, minute quantities of radio-active substances are found in some of the spring waters. Curative powers have long been ascribed to the bad-smelling slightly radio-active waters of hot springs all over the world.

You may well ask the question, Where does the water come from? To answer this, the geologist will first look to other hot springs of the world. It is now almost universally agreed that waters from springs are really surface waters that have penetrated openings and pores in the rocks, gone down to depths of several hundreds of metres, where they have been warmed and have dissolved some of the substance of the rocks themselves, and then have risen along other fractures in the rock to issue from the ground somewhere else. This origin has been established in several ways. In most places it can be shown that the amount of water issuing from springs varies with the rainfall. It has also been proven that radio-active fall-out from atomic bombs, brought into the surface waters of an area by rain, soon appears in the hot spring waters.

In Banff, the fact that there may be a delay of as much as three months—from the time the surface water enters the ground until the time it emerges in the hot spring—shows that the pool of underground water is probably large or that the path the water must trace is a long and intricate one. In some other areas though, the duration of the water's underground stay may be far greater. For example, one set of experiments done in Yellowstone National Park seems to indicate that the main body of underground water, being fed by surface waters on one end and being drawn upon to supply the hot springs at the other, probably has an average age of about 50 years. This means that it takes that long between the time the water falls as rain or snow and the time it emerges from the hot springs somewhere else, although some may pass through more quickly.

Just what fractures the water comes up seems fairly clear when one notes that the hot springs in the Banff area all seem to occur along the Sulphur Mountain fault. The source area of the water, however, is less easily found. All the rivers in the district are lower than the Upper Hot Springs so it seems unlikely that their water is the source. However, on the other side of Sulphur Mountain, Sundance Creek flows along the valley bottom at an elevation higher than the highest hot spring; and one scientist (Haites) has suggested that this stream is the original source of the water discharged by the springs at Banff. He further explains that the water must penetrate to a depth of more than 2,500 metres (8,000 feet) in its underground travels in order to reach the temperature that it does. Difference in temperature from spring to spring can be accounted for by different paths underground and also by the variation in amounts of dilution by cool surface waters.

The dissolved radium in the hot spring waters may come from certain radio-active shales that occur in the rocks of the Rocky Mountain area. The most likely candidate seems to be the Exshaw shale mentioned on page 44.

Thus, when we go swimming in the Upper Hot Springs pool or the Cave and Basin pools, let us remember that the water has had a long and interesting history between the time it passed over the land as clouds and fell as rain or snow, and the time it issued from the springs, heated and full of dissolved minerals.

Young Valleys and Old Mountains

An unusual geological feature of the east side of Banff National Park is to be found in the relationships of the rocks in the high mountains and in the valley bottoms. Experience with rocks all over the world suggests that usually the youngest layers in any sequence lie on top and the oldest ones below. This is because under ordinary circumstances rocks of a *sedimentary* origin are laid down one layer upon another. This general rule, however, does not necessarily hold true in areas of structural complexity such as the Rocky Mountains.

All the valleys on the eastern side of the Rockies in Banff National Park, and in Jasper National Park to the north, are underlain by *Cretaceous* rocks, roughly 100 million years old. The high ridges and peaks on either side of the valleys on the other hand are generally of *Devonian* age, that is, about 320 million years old. This is because the eastern Rockies, known technically as the Front Ranges, are made up of a great series of *fault slices* in which masses of rocks have been thrust eastward along sloping surfaces that allowed the moving blocks to ride up and over. Erosion into this complicated mass over the millions of years has produced the present situation where highly resistant limestone masses such as the Palliser and Rundle formations now hold up most of the peaks and ridges whereas the much softer, less-resistant younger rocks are to be found in the valley bottoms.

This arrangement is clearly seen when you travel along the valley of the Bow River south of Banff. The valley bottom is on Cretaceous rocks, with the operating coal mines at Canmore and abandoned ones at Anthracite and Bankhead at valley-bottom level, and the towering peaks of older grey limestones on each side. When you swing more westward across the trends of ridges, the Devonian limestone units come down to road level where you can often see them in road-cuts. Along the western side of the Bow Valley the Rundle-Cascade fault has brought Devonian rocks riding up and over Kootenay (Cretaceous) rocks with a movement of at least 2,500 metres (8,000 feet). Where the fault is seen, it dips or slopes westward at between 30 and 75 degrees and is generally an undulating surface. The rocks above and below the fault surface show the results of stress and movement, with the Palliser limestone above the fault being *brecciated* (broken into coarse, angular fragments) or folded. The underlying Kootenay Formation is crushed, complexly folded, and even overturned.

Thus, the young valleys and old mountains indicate a complex structural history. The forces necessary to bring about the present arrangement must have been enormous.

Old Coal Mines

In the area east of the Trans-Canada Highway between the two roads into Lake Minnewanka, you may notice piles of coaly debris, old, concrete foundations, and the remnants of old villages. These are all that mark what once were two bustling coal-mining areas within the present boundaries of Banff National Park.

Mineable coal seams occur in the Kootenay Formation, rocks of Cretaceous age, all along the east side of the Rockies, from the Panther River area southward beyond the boundaries of Banff Park to the United States border. Late in the nineteenth century and during the beginning of the twentieth, coal was mined in two places: at Anthracite, near the present main highway, and at Bankhead, about a kilometre up the northern of the two roads to Lake Minnewanka.

At Bankhead about a dozen coal beds were known, but only about half of these were worked. The coal was semi-anthracite and too hard for use on the railway, so markets were mostly in the domestic trade. In their heyday the mines at Bankhead produced some 1,020 tonnes (1,000 tons) of coal and 306 tonnes (300 tons) of briquettes a day. The mine at Anthracite worked some five seams of coal and had the same problems of market that the Bankhead area had. It was forced to close in 1904 whereas the Bankhead mines carried on till 1921.

The high mountains all around are made of Devonian and younger rocks, lying in enormous *fault slices* that were pushed up over the much younger Cretaceous rocks now found in the valleys. The coal beds all occur in the Kootenay Formation of Cretaceous age, underneath the fault surfaces. Geologists can show that in some places the coal seams probably provided the lubrication for the sliding of the great masses of rock above the fault surfaces. The movement produced severe shearing and breakage in the rocks underneath. In the mines at Bankhead and Anthracite, it was often found that the coal was almost pulverized and minor faults and slips made mining very difficult. Another effect of these *tectonic* or earth movements was that the rank or grade of the coal was raised from bituminous to semi-anthracite.

Rivers Around Banff

The most powerful agent of erosion of the land is running water in the form of rivers and streams. When you look at valleys, you may at first think that it is natural that streams flow along the valley bottom because running water flows downhill. In the late eighteenth century it became generally realized that valleys are for the most part cut by the streams that occupy them, with the moving water carrying away rocks, gravel, sand, silt, and suspended and dissolved material. Under ordinary circumstances, then, one should be able to relate the size of the river to the size of the valley, with the added reservation that the valley will change its shape as the rivers keep cutting into the land. With all this in mind, a brief look at a map of the Banff region will show some very peculiar things about the rivers and streams there.

The course of the Bow River is generally parallel to the mountains from its source at Bow Summit to a point about 10 or 11 kilometres west of Banff, where it abruptly turns eastward and cuts across the mountain ridges. This is natural enough because rivers could not flow parallel to the mountains indefinitely. Somewhere the water must cross the grain of the country and escape onto the plains on its way to the ocean. Perhaps the water first drained down the ancient valleys until it could go no farther because of a barrier, so that it was forced to form a lake. Then, as the water rose, it would eventually spill over the lowest parts of one of the ridges and gradually cut a valley across it. Maybe this is the way the eastern and northeastern parts of the Bow River valley near Banff were cut long ago. On the other hand, a fault may have cut through the rocks and made a very weak area which would rapidly be eroded by streams. Thus, a breach would have been made in the northwest-trending ridges, forming a path that the Bow River could ultimately follow.

When you follow the river farther downstream to the town of Banff, however, you will see that the Bow River turns again suddenly, this time to the southeast to flow through a narrow and fairly steep-walled valley and thence over Bow Falls. Then, instead of following the southeasterly trending valleys, it turns abruptly across the upturned edges of the massive limestone beds of Mount Rundle on the southeast and Tunnel Mountain on the northwest to resume its northeasterly course again. It flows northeasterly for only a couple

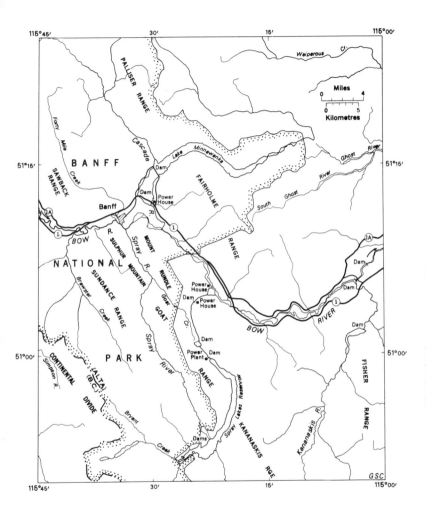

Drainage in the Banff area

59

Looking northwestward from the top of Sulphur Mountain, we see the Bow River coming in from the left and swinging abruptly across the gap between the foot of Mount Rundle (right) and Tunnel Mountain (left). The Spray River comes in parallel to the bottom right margin. In the distance a little bit of Lake Minnewanka occupies the end of the major valley that crosses the Palliser Range (left) and its extension.

of kilometres before swinging into its old southeasterly course and out of the park.

From any part of the higher ground near Banff, you can see that a very large valley seems to trend northeasterly from Banff across the mountains. A very large part of this valley is occupied now by Lake Minnewanka. If you take the trip along Lake Minnewanka to its easternmost end, you come ultimately to a flat-bottomed valley

filled with low lakes and swampy ground leading outward (eastward) toward the plains, becoming more or less continuous in some places with the valley of the present Ghost River. From Lake Minnewanka to the Ghost River, a distance of several kilometres, the valley is now occupied only by a little wash in the springtime. Look again and you will see that the Ghost River has been dammed and forced to flow westward.

For still another anomalous situation, examine the map of the area to the south and southeast of Banff for the course of the Spray River. After flowing northwestward parallel to the main ridges of the mountains for 30 kilometres or so from its source, it suddenly abandons the main trend of the valleys to cut across the ridge between Sulphur Mountain in the northwest and the Goat Range in the southeast. Then it enters another large valley, which it follows to the northwest to where it joins the Bow River just below Bow Falls at Banff. Where Spray River seems to abandon its valley and cut to the northeast, the map shows a small northwestward extension flowing between Sulphur Mountain on the east and Bourgeau Range in the west. The valley here is occupied by a very small brook, that comes back to join the Spray River in one direction, and by Sundance Creek flowing northwesterly to join the Bow River in the other. If you have gone up to the canyon of Sundance Creek, you have perhaps wondered how and why the very large valley there supports such a very small brook. How has this apparently complicated drainage pattern come about?

From all the evidence in hand it would seem that a long time ago, before the beginning of the ice age, the Bow River followed its present southeastward and then northeastward course all the way down to Banff. But at that time, instead of swinging southward through what is now Banff town and over Bow Falls, it continued to flow northeasterly out through the valleys now occupied by the lower Cascade River and Lake Minnewanka, into the Ghost River valley, and thus onto the plains. It seems likely that headward erosion by a river occupying the present Bow Valley in the general region of Canmore and the eastern park entrance gradually cut lower than, and headward into, the old Bow River valley, capturing the main drainage from it. This, then, left the old valley high and dry with only a few remnant lakes and swamps and small brooks running in it.

When glaciers covered the area very thickly, they brought great amounts of rock waste from the mountains and valleys around. When the ice melted, huge quantities of debris were left behind in the valley bottoms and washed out from the melting ice. A particularly large mass of this material filled the glaciated valley where the old Bow Valley and the new one came together. At one stage, a plug in the valley pushed the Bow River out of its course so that it flowed southeastward along a kilometre or two of what must have been the ancestral Goat Creek near its junction with the old Bow River. It is probable that a considerable lake was backed up into the Bow River valley when this happened. The water eventually spilled over at the rock gap between Tunnel Mountain and the end of Mount Rundle. This gap was cut progressively lower until now there is very little barrier to the water of Bow River there. Also during the glacial period, the old river valley of the Bow River farther to the east was filled with glacial debris and the ancestor of Lake Minnewanka was formed. This drained generally westward to join the Bow River, reversing the drainage in that part of the valley of the Bow.

Meanwhile similar things were happening to the Spray River. Sometime during its history, water began to cut through the ridge now marked by the Goat Range on the one hand and Sulphur Mountain on the other until a cross valley was formed. This may have been done during one of the several glacial periods when either ice or sand and gravel blocked the old valley now occupied by Sundance Creek and Sundance Pass.

When you look at the Vermilion Lakes and the winding, twisting course of the Bow River on the valley flat at and above Banff, you are looking at a valley partly filled with glacial deposits. Some of this may be in the old lake bottom that we mentioned earlier.

In his quest for hydro-electric energy, man has drastically altered the natural drainage of the area, complicated in its history as it is. The headwaters of the Ghost River, for example, have been dammed nearly opposite the eastern end of Lake Minnewanka and the water diverted into that lake. This means that Ghost River water now passes through three power plants, two on the Bow and one near the junction of the Bow and the Ghost, instead of just the last one as it would had this diversion not been put in.

Lake Minnewanka itself has been raised between 18 and 20 metres by the dam at its western end to form a magnificent reservoir, which can be drawn on as desired.

The Spray River hydro-electric development is interesting in a geological sense because the main dam across the canyon of the Spray River has made a very large lake, now called Spray Reservoir, which occupies the site of an old natural lake. This was formed when glaciers dammed earlier drainage lines with piles of gravel and debris. Within the last few thousands of years the Spray River, cutting a new course, eroded headward into the glacial debris and thence down into the underlying rock to drain the natural lake and to divert the drainage of the area into the Spray River and then into the Bow at Banff. All that was left of the very large lake were two small ones, the Upper and Lower Spray lakes, and a few pools in the small stream between them. Thus, the hydro-electric dam on the upper Spray River literally beheads the river and turns the water eastward to where it used to flow in the upper part of Goat Creek. However, another dam there diverts the water along a canal, Whiteman's Pass, and then into the Bow River. A total drop of 335 metres (1,100 feet) is achieved through this most interesting system of dams, reversal of drainage, and raising of reservoir areas.

Thus, you can see that the drainage of an area is not as simple as the idea that water naturally flows in the bottoms of the valleys. The Banff area shows abundant evidence of having had a very involved drainage history, with numerous changes back and forth owing to the movement of mountain masses and, more recently, because of a complicated glacial history. And now man, with his dams and his canals, further alters the natural flow of running water.

Now, when you sit beside the quiet moving, green waters of the Bow River at Banff townsite, or hear the roar of Bow Falls, or even as you drive along the empty valley near the airport between the two Banff cloverleafs, you may find it fascinating to think of the ancient mountains and the long periods of erosion when the valleys were being carved and, in recent times, of the changing of the river systems.

This lovely tarn lies in its rockbound
basin behind Mount Eisenhower,
as seen from the highway.

Mount Eisenhower

Great walls of Precambrian and Cambrian rocks *(right)* mark the top of the front of Mount Eisenhower, but at the back *(below)* a high-level valley with woods and lakes opens to the southward towards Banff and the Bow Valley. In winter the famous castellated mountain looms beautifully into the winter sky.

Mount Temple is really the end of a
ridge between Moraine Valley to the left
and Paradise Valley to the right.

Lake Louise lies in a glacial basin high
above the valley of the Bow River, with
glacier-covered Mount Victoria at the back.

Opposite:
Slates at the junction of the Trans-
Canada and Banff-Jasper highways.

Below:
Rivers flowing eastwards from the
mountains out onto the plains fill their
valleys with sand and gravel, the waste
of eroding mountains. This is the Red
Deer River.

Above: Bow Lake and Crowfoot Glacier.

Mount Drummond
Great cliffs of limestone and shaly slopes lead from the wooded valleys to snow-capped summits in the remote Cataract Peak area, about twenty kilometres northeast of Hector Lake on the Banff-Jasper highway.

Opposite:
Alpine meadows and scattered patches
of woods lie in front of a glacial bowl
cut into the mass of Panther Mountain
in the eastern part of the park, about
thirty kilometres north of Banff.

Below:
Bulging masses of ice are draped over
the rocks in the Mount Drummond
area twenty kilometres east of Hector
Lake on the Banff-Jasper highway.

Below:
Brown and grey limestones with shaly slopes between, near Cataract Peak.

Opposite:
Most of the year this lake is tightly frozen, but in the few months of summer it makes a turquoise gem in the lee of Cataract Peak.

Mount Wilson
The various peaks of Mount Wilson hide a glacier-covered back from viewers along the middle section of the Banff-Jasper highway. The white stream, just above centre, gushes from an opening in the mountain, having started in the meltwaters on the other side.

In summer this boisterous torrent leaps
and tumbles over the rocks opposite
the road on the gravel flat below Parker
Ridge. It comes from the melting
snow and ice on the northern slope of
Mount Saskatchewan.

Roadlogs and Points of Interest

As you drive through Banff National Park you pass a number of viewpoints, camping spots, parking areas, and other places where the view is especially good or where there are things of special scenic and geological interest. What you can see from each of these places is described here in a series of roadlogs, and the numbered stops can be followed on the maps facing pages 64 and 208.

For convenience, the roadlogs are divided into these sections: (I) Trans-Canada Highway from the eastern park entrance to the Banff cloverleaf; (II) Banff and vicinity; (III) Trans-Canada Highway from Banff to Eisenhower Junction; (IV) the road from Eisenhower Junction to Vermilion Pass and Kootenay National Park; (V) Trans-Canada Highway from Eisenhower Junction to Lake Louise Junction; (VI) Lake Louise and Moraine Lake; (VII) Trans-Canada Highway from Lake Louise Junction to Kicking Horse Pass and Yoho National Park and back along the old highway to Lake Louise; (VIII) the old highway (now Route 1A) from Lake Louise Junction to near Banff; (IX) Banff-Jasper highway from Lake Louise Junction to Bow Pass; (X) Banff-Jasper highway from Bow Pass to North Saskatchewan River crossing; (XI) Banff-Jasper highway from North Saskatchewan River crossing to Sunwapta Pass and Jasper National Park.

Some people will be travelling in the same direction as the roadlog so that they can follow the sequence in this book directly. Others will be driving in the opposite direction and therefore will have to use the logs in reverse and travel downward in number from locality to locality. The approximate driving distance between adjacent stops is given between the sections describing them.

81

Marvel Lake, with its small satellite, Terrapin Lake, lies in a great bowl amid rugged mountains which include Mount Assiniboine, the main peak in the centre background. The nearly horizontal rock layers are characteristic of this area.

Roadlog I
Trans-Canada Highway from Eastern Park Entrance to Banff Cloverleaf

1 Main Southeast Entrance

The facilities of the main eastern entrance to Banff National Park and the road on either side are built on sand and gravel deposits on the valley flats of the Bow River. An old meandering sweep of the Bow River is visible through the screen of trees just to the south and you may see where it has been dyked off to prevent flooding during the spring high water. To the west and southwest, the steep reverse side of Mount Rundle shows the upturned edges of great layers of limestone and shale. The topmost jagged line of the mountain is made of limestone of the Rundle Formation of Mississippian age, about 330 million years old. Below it is a brownish-weathering shale, the Banff shale, also of Mississippian age. The lower cliffs of Mount Rundle are formed by the massive Palliser limestone which is Devonian in age, nearly 400 million years old. Older rocks are exposed here and there along the foot of the mountain.

Away to the east and northeast (to the right as you enter the park) the grey limestone of Mount Charles Stewart is interrupted by the valley of Carrot Creek to the northwest and then the peak of Mount Peechee. The rocks in both these peaks dip westward toward the Bow River valley, along which the highway is located. Straight up the valley to the northwest looms the bulk of Cascade Mountain.

From where you stand, the park boundary is visible to the west on the slopes of Mount Rundle as a faint scar cutting straight through the woods. Directly opposite this viewpoint the topmost rocks belong to the Banff Formation of Mississippian age. Below that the yellow-grey cliffs are of the thick Palliser limestone of Devonian age. This is underlain by rocks of the Fairholme Group in the wooded slopes below the cliffs. The much older limestone, of Cambrian age, forms a low cliff along the top of the bottom wooded slope. Ahead, along the main highway, the first hill leads up onto a higher terrace of gravels deposited by the glaciers—the same gravels that floor the valley of the Bow River here.

To Stop 2—2.4 kilometres (1.5 miles)

2 Carrot Creek Crossing, South Side of Bridge

Westward, the back of Mount Rundle exposes the upturned edges of three of the great rock formations of the Rocky Mountains: the Rundle limestone on the very crest of the mountain, the brown-weathering Banff shale below, and the great cliff-forming Palliser limestone of Devonian age, forming the jutting prow of massive rock just above the forests opposite. Ahead and to the northwest, Cascade Mountain shows the same three formations wrinkled into a *syncline* or downfold on the left, and an *anticline* or upfold on the right, with westward dips beyond.

On the right, the bank of glacial debris is made up of partly rounded boulders which are mostly of grey limestone. This bank is being cut into by the stream, and as the boulders continue on down river they will be made even rounder by the bumping and grinding action as they move along. Here and there in the banks you can see a layering or bedding in the gravels, showing their water-washed origin. In some places the surface of the ground clearly is part of three different levels or terraces, displaying where Carrot Creek has cut into it at different levels at different times.

Far up Carrot Creek to the northeast, complicated fold structures are visible in the mountains, as is the westward dip of the near slopes of the Fairholme Range. Mount Charles Stewart lies to the right of the valley and Mount Princess Margaret to the left.

To Stop 3—2.7 kilometres (1.7 miles)

3 Roadside Stop at Picnic Area, Between Two Big Bends in Road

The highway skirts along the edge of a terrace of the Bow River with the new Trans-Canada Highway having been relocated back from the edge a few metres. From the wayside tables on the old road close to the edge of the terrace, the flat of the Bow River is clearly shown, with the steep banks leading down to where the river itself is cutting into the sand and gravel, probably placed there originally as material from the glaciers. Across the valley are the lower slopes of Mount Rundle, with a Y-shaped gash made by snowslides in the wooded slopes below the yellow-grey cliffs of the Palliser limestone. This great limestone layer clearly dips or slopes to the west, away from where you stand. From here the ridge of Mount Rundle stretches away for many kilometres to the southeast.

The Fairholme Range extends along the other side of the valley, and strong westward dips in the grey limestone units are visible in the cross valley opposite. A bit of Cascade Mountain is visible over the tree tops from here. More to the west, the wooded lower slopes of Mount Norquay are interrupted by the very green grassy clearings, which are ski areas in wintertime. The small wooded lump in mid-valley is Tunnel Mountain. Banff town lies just beyond and below it.

To Stop 4 — 3.4 kilometres (2.1 miles)

4 Roadside Stop Opposite Pillars of Glacial Debris at Picnic Area and Turnoff

Cliffs of glacial debris that accumulated here as outwash deposits from melting glaciers in the main valley and the side valleys are often eroded into tall pillars by the rain as it gullies into the steep banks. The pillars form only under special circumstances. In the first place, a considerable thickness of semi-con-

The great quantity of waste in the bowl surrounding the end of Lake Gloria comes partly from the scree and talus and partly as wash from glaciers, past and present. Mount Aye is at the right, Mount Eon just left of centre, and a spur from Mount Gloria at left.

---

solidated or partly-cemented sand, clay, and boulders seems to be needed. Secondly, a steep cliff-maker such as a brook or river must cut into this material at a low level to make a vertical wall, otherwise the erosion is more or less even and the whole mass slacks off in gentle round slopes.

Right below the pillared cliffs is the first primitive road through this part of Banff National Park. Approximately one and a half metres to the west the next improved road was made, and now the new Trans-Canada Highway has been located still west of that.

To the south of here, Mount Rundle extends in a scarp or steep slope for many kilometres. To the northwest, the folding in the mass of Cascade Mountain is clearly seen, with an anticline or upfold on the left, a syncline or downfold in the centre, and another anticline on the right side.

To Stop 5—1.3 kilometres (0.8 mile)

5 Junction of Lake Minnewanka Road

From this road junction the view southward shows a magnificent procession of jagged ridges along the crest of the Rundle Range on the west side of the Bow Valley. Here and there are glimpses of the Fairholme Range on the eastern side of the valley. Northwestward, straight up the road, the great mass of Cascade Mountain looms across the view with three deep gashes in its lower limestone cliffs. The left one has a thin white ribbon of falling water and it is from this that the mountain gets its name. The main grey cliff in the bottom is the Palliser limestone of Devonian age. Above it, slacking off into more gentle, rounded, brownish slopes is the Banff shale formation of Mississippian age. The top of the mountain is in the grey, cliff-forming Rundle limestone, also of Mississippian age. It is the same threefold Palliser-Banff-Rundle sequence that is seen in so many mountains up and down the length of Banff National Park. To the west, is Mount Norquay, along with several of the sharp peaks of the Sawback Range.

The Lake Minnewanka road cuts up through the gravelly terrace to the next level. Here and there along the road are old piles of coal and coal waste, reminders that this was once the coal-mining area that supplied the railways coming through this valley in the early part of the century. The small power-house about half a kilometre to the north along the road from this stop is made of stone taken from the Spray River Formation in the Banff area. Water to turn the generators comes from the Lake Minnewanka area to the northeast. Its diversion to this area is a man-made change in the drainage, the latest in a long history of drainage changes that affected the whole of this area (see page 63).

To Stop 6—2.2 kilometres (1.4 miles)

6 Stop Beside Jagged Rock Outcrops

Two separate areas of outcropping shales of Cretaceous age, with limy and sandy beds sticking out sharply, occur in the main road a little more than half a kilometre apart. These make a most interesting rock pattern and, in addition, show something of the structure of the whole of this valley, for these rocks are very much younger than the rocks in the mountains on all sides. Now, under ordinary circumstances, one

At several places along the roadside between the eastern park entrance and the Banff cloverleaf, banks of partly consolidated glacial debris crop out. Here, erosion is cutting deeply into the cliff, and hoodoos are being made.

would expect younger rocks to be laid down on top of older rocks according to the *law of superposition,* as explained on page 35.

Detailed geological mapping along the base of Cascade Mountain, including the great grey mass you see to the northwest of this area

Lake Minnewanka lies in the valley that cuts directly across the structure of the mountains east of Banff. The dam in the foreground has raised the level of the lake. Mount Inglismaldie looms high to the right.

and the lower slopes to the right or east as you face it, shows that the Mississippian and Devonian aged rocks have been uplifted and thrust over the Cretaceous rocks along an irregular surface not far below the lower grey limestone cliff of the mountain. One cannot help but feel pretty feeble when thinking of the enormous forces that must have been necessary to squeeze and push the outer layers of the earth's crust to move these tremendous masses of rock and slide them up one over another. And even then, what one now sees in Cascade Mountain is only a much-eroded remnant of a larger mass.

The coal mines that gave the name to the extinct village of Anthracite are now seen only as a few old foundations and heaps of coaly waste a little way up the Cascade River. The coal occurred in the Cretaceous rocks, and in some of the mine workings the rocks were found to be very much broken and sheared as one would expect close to a major *thrust fault* surface. You can see how close you must be to the actual fault surface by noting the Cretaceous outcrops on the road and a small outcrop of Devonian limestone along the railway.

To Stop 7 — approximately
1.6 kilometres (1 mile)

7 Banff Cloverleaf

You may have noted that the Cascade River is now very much shrunken where the road crosses it. This is because the water from this drainage system now passes largely through the canals and flumes to the power plant that you pass on the main highway a little to the south of here.

On the north side of the cloverleaf, the Banff airport is built on the gravelly flats of the old river valley system. Southward lies Mount Rundle with its very conspicuous three layers, the grey Palliser cliffs on the lower side, the brownish-weathering Banff shale above, and the Rundle limestone on top.

Beyond the dark forested lump of Tunnel Mountain is Sulphur Mountain, with others showing in the dis-

tance to the west up the Bow Valley. The great slopes of Cascade Mountain are directly to the north, and here again is displayed the great threefold rock sandwich — the Palliser-Banff-Rundle layers — so common in the eastern Rockies.

To the east, complicated rock structures are visible in the Palliser Range. Lake Minnewanka lies between this spot and the straight rock wall above the wooded slope to the east. As you face east, the gap made by Lake Minnewanka's valley leads up and to the right to the peak of Mount Inglismaldie, then around a great bowl, at the back of which is Mount Girouard, and finally to the layered and curved peak of Mount Peechee. A well-marked upper terrace shows eastward along the road and under the mass of Mount Inglismaldie and Mount Peechee.

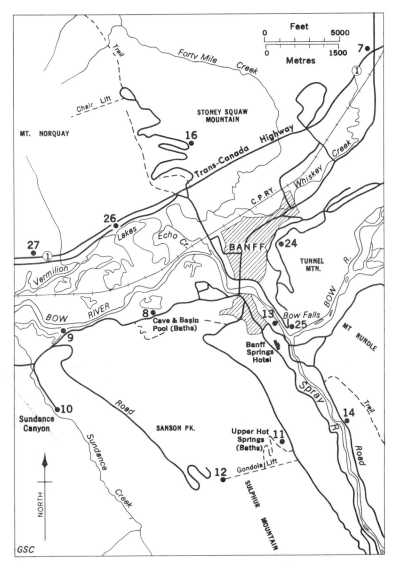

Enlargement of Banff Area

90

Roadlog II
In and Around Banff

DRIVE TO SUNDANCE CANYON AND FALLS, INCLUDING THE CAVE AND BASIN POOL

Bow River bridge in Banff to Cave and Basin Pool—1.8 kilometres (1.1 miles)

8 Cave and Basin Pool Area

The hot springs that issue from the limestones of Sulphur Mountain in this area have largely been covered with the swimming and bathing facilities of the Cave and Basin Pool area. When first discovered by workers on the Canadian Pacific Railway in the 1880s, the hot springs issued from the rocks and spilled out among the woods, invisible from a distance in the summer but marked by clouds of steam in winter. One of the original openings of the springs, however, has been preserved; and you may go in to see it along a partly man-made and partly natural tunnel on the Banff side of the built-up area. Here, at the end of the very hot moist cavern, the hot water springs from deep inside the earth. At several places around the pool buildings, spongy rock deposits mark the precipitation of dissolved limestone from the spring waters over the centuries.

The building stone used in the buildings and walks in this neighbourhood has all come from the Spray River quarry, where thin-bedded rocks of Triassic age crop out along the river banks.

The hot springs in the Banff area are discussed fully on pages 52 to 55.

To Stop 9—1.6 kilometres (1.0 mile)

9 Roadside Stop Beside Backwater of Bow River

From here, right at water level, a superb view of the end of the Sawback Range is presented to you across the flats on the bottom of the Bow River valley. The rocks in the Sawbacks stick up almost vertically, making very sharp, toothlike peaks, as you can see in the steep pinnacle of Mount Edith which thrusts itself skyward directly opposite you amid other peaks of more gentle outline. It is this jagged skyline appearance, seen more from the side than as you see it here from the end, that gives the Sawback mountain range its name. To the right as you look across the river (or eastward), Cascade Mountain presents great slabby slopes of grey limestone on the near limb of an *anticline* or upfold with the rocks dipping toward you. Opposite you the double grey peak is Mount Norquay, with a 60-degree westward slope showing conspicuously in the grey limestones. Away down the river Mount In-

glismaldie, with Mount Girouard just to the right, shows on the distant skyline. Up river a whole array of mountains presents a tumbled appearance. Just in front Bow River flows gently by, carrying finely suspended rock material that may ultimately come to rest in Hudson Bay, thousands of kilometres to the east.

To Stop 10 — 1.9 kilometres (1.2 miles)

10   Sundance Canyon and Falls

The rocks in the bottom of the valley of Sundance Creek dip sharply to the west. The creek has eroded down a soft layer rather rapidly at its lower end, making thus a steep-walled canyon with an overhanging wall following the westerly dip on one side and the parallel but ordinary dip slope on the other. Because of the undercutting, large boulders have fallen off the overhanging wall, and it is over these that the waters of Sundance Creek tumble in a series of cascades.

Opposite, above: Sunlight casts shadows on a lightly rippled surface of the Spray River Formation in this quarry about three kilometres southeast of Banff. Millions of years ago this surface was the floor of the sea, and waves and currents made these marks. Sundance Creek *(below)*, which flows into the Bow River a few kilometres west of Banff, runs through a narrow gorge. A footpath leads alongside it.

The most intriguing thing about this area is that in distant times some much larger rivers came through this valley. Now, however, the upper drainage has been tapped by the Spray River which cuts across the mountain some distance to the southeast, capturing the waters that used to flow down the Sundance Valley. This is just one of the many strange events that mark the drainage history of the Banff area, described fully on pages 57 to 64.

SULPHUR MOUNTAIN, INCLUDING THE UPPER HOT SPRINGS AREA

Bow River bridge in Banff to Upper Hot Springs parking lot — 3.7 kilometres (2.3 miles)

11   Upper Hot Springs Pool Area

As you walk from the parking lot up to the Upper Hot Springs pool bathing facilities, you will note banks of a spongy rock sometimes soaked in warm water on the uphill side of the road. This spongy rock has been deposited around the hot springs in times past as the orifices or outlets appeared on the surface at different places and at different times. Now, much of the hot water is captured and put through pipes to end up in the hot springs pool; it is disposed of farther down the mountainside through pipes, thus interrupting the ordinary deposition that might still be taking place.

You may note once again that the buildings in this area, like most of the other public buildings in Banff National Park, are built of flat angular blocks of rock from the quarry a short distance up the Spray River from Banff.

12   Top of Sulphur Mountain

The crest of Sulphur Mountain supplies a superb view of the mountains, the valleys, and the rivers of the whole Banff area. Directly below to the east is the valley of the Spray River on the right, joining that of the Bow on the left, with the combined waters swinging through the gap in the mountains to the northeast before turning out of sight behind the shoulder of Mount Rundle. Above the water gap in the distance is seen a bit of Lake Minnewanka in its major valley, cutting across the trend of the mountains (the Palliser Range to the north or left, and the Fairholme Range to the south or right). The very high peak in the distance, above and just left of the end of Lake Minnewanka, is Mount Aylmer, 3,164 metres (10,375 feet) above sea level. To the right of the Lake Minnewanka

The view southwestward from the summit of Sulphur Mountain across the valley of Sundance Creek shows the top of the Bourgeau Range with a bowl-shaped depression, or cirque, at the head of each of the valleys.

gap are, first, Mount Inglismaldie at 2,966 metres (9,725 feet) above sea level, near it Mount Girouard at 2,996 metres (9,825 feet), and then a long snowy rock wall leading still farther to the right to Mount Peechee at 2,936 metres (9,625 feet), showing a gentle northward dip (down and to the left) in its rock structure. As you swing your view a little farther to the right, the great dip slopes of grey limestone of the Rundle Formation lead up to the serrated edge and peak of Mount Rundle itself. The Spray River valley stretches away to the right or south.

Below you again and just above the Banff Springs Hotel you may note the short canyon and falls of the Bow River, and behind that the peculiar isolated lump of limestone — Tunnel Mountain. Just above the left or northern lump at the top of Tunnel Mountain, you can see the scars made through the forests by the main highways, the railway, and the airport. These are built on gravelly flats which have been cut into by the various streams of the region. This is visible in the terraced effect between the water gap of the Bow River in the foreground and Lake Minnewanka in the background.

Looking still more to the north or left, you can see the great bulk of Cascade Mountain, its lower cliffs made of Palliser limestone, its more subdued intermediate slopes of Banff shale, and its crest cut into limestones of the Rundle Formation. The next mountain to the north is Mount Norquay, with green patches in summer marking areas cleared for winter skiing.

A view westward from the crest shows the heavily wooded valley of Sundance Creek leading upward to the mountains of the Sundance Range, whose bare summits are incised by a series of bowllike depressions or *cirques,* reminders of the time when glaciers were more extensive in this area.

As you walk down the trail toward the end of the ridge where the experimental station is situated, you will discover a superb view to the northwest over the valley of the Bow River. Far below on the valley floor the Bow River twists and turns in its serpentine course before heading southeastward into the village of Banff. The Vermilion Lakes are clearly backwaters on the flat alluvial plain. The end of the Sawback Range, including Mount Norquay directly across the valley, bounds the valley of the Bow River on the east.

SPRAY RIVER AND GOLF COURSE LOOP DRIVE

Bow River bridge in Banff to Bow Falls parking area — 1.6 kilometres (1.0 mile)

13 Bow Falls Parking Area

In earlier times, Bow River flowed northeastward past the present site of Banff to join the ancestor of the Cascade River before turning southeastward into what is now the lower Bow River valley. Now, because of changes in the level of the land, mostly by the addition of material dumped by the glaciers, the Bow River flows abruptly southeast from the old river valley for a short distance, then turns sharply northeast below the present position of Bow Falls. Here, it cuts through the ridge made by Mount Rundle and Tunnel Mountain in a steep-sided water gap before turning to the southeast to join the Cascade River and the lower Bow Valley. The Spray River, too, has had a complicated history and may actually have been the first to flow through the Tunnel Mountain—Mount Rundle water gap.

The general history of drainage changes in the Banff area is described in more detail on page 58. It is important here only to realize that the part of the Bow River you see plunging over Bow Falls and through the narrow valley just above it is a very recent drainage feature.

As you stand below the falls looking upstream, the rocks on the right are of *Palaeozoic* age—between about 240 million and 600 million years old. They form the uppermost part of a sequence that includes both Mount Rundle and Tunnel Mountain. The rocks on the left, on the other hand, are of the more recent *Mesozoic* era and belong to the Spray River Group, having been formed or laid down in the Triassic period, about 200 million years ago. The river flows along the contact between rock groups of different ages. The fact that it takes this course is no accident, because along such contacts the rocks are often more easily eroded than elsewhere.

At one time the Bow Falls were probably very much higher than they are now. As you look at the falls you will notice a series of steep rapids extending for several hundred metres above them. It seems fairly certain that when the waters of the Bow River first flowed this way, they plunged over a cliff almost as high as the present left bank at the falls themselves and that over the thousands of years they have gradually cut down the rock barrier to the present level. As time goes on we can expect the rocks at the falls, and those just above them, to be eroded more rapidly because of the fast-moving water. Thus, the quiet stretches of the Bow River near Banff may once again flow more swiftly when this rock barrier has been removed.

Just below the falls you will see where the Spray River joins the Bow. The quantity of water brought in by the Spray is very modest in-

Above: In this view of the Bow Falls, the rocks seen on the left are of the Spray River Formation, of Triassic age. It is from rocks of this formation that much of the building stone is quarried a little south of Banff for the administrative buildings, monuments, gateways and other structures in the park. *Below:* Blocks of fine-grained argillite of the Spray River Formation form the post office wall.

deed because its headwaters have been cut off in a hydro-electric development that drains the water through a system of canals and power flumes into the Bow River near Canmore. A brief glance at a map of the southern part of Banff Park will show that the Spray River is a very peculiar one, rising as it does in a series of streams that pour into a valley (now occupied by the Spray Reservoir) that cuts across the trend of the mountains. The water used to drain generally north-westward along a fairly large open valley, then suddenly abandoning that valley to flow directly across the trend of the mountain ridges—Sulphur Mountain in the northwest and the Goat Range in the south-east—to flow in a valley that really belongs to Goat Creek. This it follows northeastward to where you see it joining the Bow River. A more detailed story of drainage in this area is given on pages 57 to 64.

14   Spray River Quarry

A quarry has been cut into the rocks of the Spray River Group of Triassic age on the right bank of the Spray River (always as you look down-stream) about one and a half kilometres above the bridge at Bow Falls. Various footpaths, horse trails, and fire roads lead along both sides of the Spray River, making the quarry accessible in many ways. At the quarry there is a series of steeply

dipping layers of dark-coloured, dense siltstones, which may be from 2 centimetres to 9 or 10 centimetres thick, interlayered with shales. The siltstones break easily into blocks of a useful size for building purposes, and it is these that have been used very widely in the buildings in western national parks. You can see them in the Banff Springs Hotel, the Administration Building at the headquarters area in Banff, in the Banff Post Office, and the various buildings at the southeastern park entrance.

When the sun is high you will be able to see, on the bedding surfaces of these rocks, various patterns which suggest ripple marks and mud cracks. Both indicate that the rocks were formed in shallow water; the mud cracks even suggest that they were exposed to the atmosphere. Cracks would form by shrinkage in drying muds exposed perhaps at low tide in the ancient seas that once covered this district. This is the same rock group that is visible in road-cuts at Stop No. 6 near the Lake Minnewanka turnoff on the main highway and again near the Vermilion Lakes viewpoints (Stop No. 26) on the highway west of Banff.

15   Golf Course and Loop Drive

A leisurely drive around the golf course and the loop on the end of the road takes you under the cliffs

99

that form the northeastern end of Mount Rundle. In the woods you will see great limestone boulders which have fallen from the hills above. Some have been there for hundreds of years while others may have come down very recently. The more open parts of the road around the loop are built on the flat at the bottom of the valley of the present Bow River. On the outside of the turn close to the Bow River, you can look across at the steep banks of fine sand and gravel into which the Bow River is cutting as it changes course from northeast to southeast. It is in some of these banks that the peculiar pillars or *hoodoos* are cut. These form when the consistency of the sands and gravels is just right and when the cliffs are steep enough that rain and melting snow eat into the banks, isolating the pillars.

MOUNT NORQUAY DRIVE

A drive of about 6 kilometres (a little less than 4 miles) on a looping switchback road takes you from the overpass and cloverleaf at the west end of Banff to a flat area partly up the southeast slopes of Mount Norquay. From the top of this drive a chair lift goes farther up Mount Norquay for wintertime skiing on the same slopes that you see now and again as grassy green areas in summer. The view from the top of the chair lift, however, offers little more than that from the parking areas on the outsides of some of the hairpin turns on the way up.

16   Upper Hairpin Turn and Viewpoint

From here, a lovely view out over the valley of the Bow River to the south and southeast shows the ends of the mountain ranges crossed by the Bow River valley. To the right are the steeply westward dipping rocks of the Sundance Range and the wooded round-bottomed valley of Sundance Creek. These lie on the right of the sharp-crested Sulphur Mountain. The bare peak is made of the Rundle limestone of Mississippian age. The wooded slopes of Sulphur Mountain are mostly on rocks of the Banff Formation. Farther to the left, beyond the open *U* of the Spray River valley, you can again see the grey limestone slopes of the Rundle Formation, which in turn overlies the Banff Formation, and beneath that the Palliser limestone in Mount Rundle. These rock layers are repeated because *faulting* has pushed great blocks of these rock units from the depths of the earth up and over younger rocks. This is why Triassic rocks of the Spray River Group are found in the bottom of the valley and the older rocks are found making these great west-dipping ridges that from here can be seen stretching off in the distance to the south, like windrows in a hayfield.

The Spray River can be seen cutting through the ridge, the near end of which is Sulphur Mountain and the far part, the Goat Range. From here you can appreciate perhaps more easily how the Spray River at one time came straight on through the Sundance Valley, where Sundance Creek now flows, to join the ancestral Bow River above what we now call Sulphur Mountain. Beyond the conspicuous gap, the Goat Range extends away to the south, with some quite high peaks showing.

The outstanding part of any scene looking toward Banff from this area must be Mount Rundle's magnificent dip slopes, formed on the bedding or layered surfaces of the Rundle limestone, with its jagged peak made on the broken edge of that massive rock unit. Below it to the left, the softer slopes of the Banff shale on the east scarp give way eventually to the great cliffs formed by the Palliser limestone underneath. Below, on the valley floor, the lump of Tunnel Mountain beyond and to the left of the village of Banff shows the looping scar of the Tunnel Mountain road. The Upper Hot Springs area is visible just above the Banff Springs Hotel and the Cave and Basin Springs area is visible at the foot of Sulphur Mountain. On the valley flat, below, the Bow River with its green waters passes along the far side of the valley beyond the dark Vermilion Lakes, which are flooded flats on the valley bottom. The reason for the sharp difference in the colour of the water is because of the suspended matter picked up by the moving waters of the Bow in its headwaters below the glaciers and in outwash areas high in its headwaters. The suspended matter reflects light. Where such water has a chance to stand still for a while, the suspended matter gradually settles out and the water becomes darker in general appearance because the light can penetrate farther, or even to the bottom.

The course of the Bow River to the east is abruptly altered, as you can see from here, by the sharp bend to the southeast. This new course is again interrupted by a right-angled bend to the northeast just beyond the village of Banff where the Bow cuts through the water gap beyond Tunnel Mountain. It is easy to think of the Bow River continuing on northeastward in earlier times. With all these features, combined with what you can see of the Spray River valley and its peculiarities, you can begin to realize what a complicated history the drainage must have had in this region.

LOOP DRIVE TO LAKE MINNEWANKA, RETURNING VIA THE HOODOOS AND TUNNEL MOUNTAIN

Proceed from the centre of Banff to the overpass and cloverleaf at the western entrance via the Trans-Canada Highway, to the Banff cloverleaf beyond the airport and to the Lake Minnewanka turnoff there. Return via the southeastern leg of the Lake Minnewanka loop to the Trans-Canada Highway, eastward to the road junction marked Tunnel Mountain Campground, and along the Tunnel Mountain drive to the central part of Banff village again.

Bow River bridge to western Banff entrance on Trans-Canada Highway—1.8 kilometres (1.1 miles)

Western Banff entrance on Trans-Canada Highway to Banff cloverleaf (this is Stop 7 described earlier)—4.3 kilometres (2.7 miles)

From cloverleaf on Trans-Canada Highway, along Lake Minnewanka road, to crossing of brook off Cascade Mountain— 1.4 kilometres (0.9 mile)

17 Brook Crossing

This brook begins high on Cascade Mountain and comes tumbling off the steep slopes in a deeply cut gash in the massive cliff of the Palliser limestone formation. At the highway the brook cuts into a great mass of light grey limestone boulders and

cobbles that it has brought down itself from higher up. Highway maintenance people try to confine the brook to its present channel, but you can see all around you indications that sometimes it spreads out over the surrounding area. What a tremendous gush of water this brook must be during spring and early summer floods!

In Cascade Mountain, above the great Palliser cliff, you can see the brownish Banff shale and some of the peak cut in the Rundle limestone high above. Peaks of the Palliser Range show to the east. One of the entrances to the old coal mine area joins the Lake Minnewanka road only a hundred metres or so beyond here.

From brook crossing to side road to coal mine, near monument on right and old foundation opposite gravel bank

To Stop 18—approximately 1.6 kilometres (1 mile)

18 Old Coal Mine Area

Between Stops 17 and 18 you have probably seen some of the old foundations of buildings and had glimpses on the right or south side of piles of waste from the old coal mines that flourished in this area in the early part of the century. The side road here is easy to miss, so watch for the monument on one

Rusting iron, decaying concrete, and piles of oxidizing waste are all that mark the once thriving town of Anthracite about five kilometres east of Banff in the valley of the Cascade River.

side of the road and an old foundation. The road leads abruptly downhill to the right. A few hundred metres off the highway down this road there is an area where men once laboured and planned, but where now next to nothing is left to mark their passing. Where once the chuffing of steam machinery and shouts of men mingled with natural sounds, there is now only the roar of distant brooks and the soughing of the wind in the trees and the grass. The site of former mining buildings and business offices is now one of only a few rusting masses of iron amid weathering concrete.

Cascade Mountain, and Mount Rundle which is more or less in line with it, consist of huge masses of Devonian and Mississippian rocks that dip steeply to the west, having been thrust up from the depths of

the earth and pushed over much younger shales and siltstones of Triassic and Cretaceous age found now only in the lower levels of the valley. In the Cretaceous rocks, thin seams of coal mark the accumulation of vast quantities of plant debris in ancient swamps and forests that covered this area about 100 million years ago. From these seams, in what is called the Kootenay Formation, coal is still mined at Canmore, a few kilometres outside the eastern entrance to Banff National Park and in the Crowsnest Pass area far to the south. Here, on the site of the old villages of Bankhead and Anthracite, these coal beds, from 60 centimetres to more than 2 metres thick, supplied many thousands of tonnes of coal for the railway at about the turn of the century. Difficulties underground with much faulted and broken coal, combined with labour trouble and a diminishing market, caused the shut-down and abandonment of the mines, and the villages soon melted away.

To Stop 19—0.8 kilometre (0.5 mile)

Opposite: The steep valley walls of some of the small streams that cross the structures of the Palliser Range show that the mountains there are underlain by intricately folded and faulted rocks. An anticline, or upfold, is clearly exposed in cross section on this steep valley wall.

19   Roadside, Top of Hill

This section of the road to Lake Minnewanka is on an *eskery* glacial bank for several hundred metres. *Eskers* are made under great tongues of ice when crevasses or underground river channels become filled with sand and gravel. When the ice disappears the deposit forms an embankmentlike, sinuous ridge such as the one you are now on. All the boulders and cobbles in the roadside here have been rounded by running water.

Visible in the woods high on the hillside to the left are piles of waste from an old coal shaft. On quiet days the distant roar of the numerous brooks coming off Cascade Mountain can be heard clearly. The Bow Valley extends into the distance southeastward. More or less ahead along the road, the valley now occupied by Lake Minnewanka forms a gap between the mountains of the Palliser Range on the left (or north) and those of the Fairholme Range on the right (or south). The sweeping dip slopes of the bare limestones in Mount Rundle contrast with Sulphur Mountain's wooded slopes, topped by the light grey limestone only at the very peak. The Sundance Range shows brownish beyond. Looming above you are Cascade's great limestone slopes and cliffs. The wooded slopes below the limestone cliffs are underlain mostly by Cretaceous shale.

*Roadside stop to road junction —
2.1 kilometres (1.3 miles)*

*Junction to end of road and
beginning of Stewart Canyon
trail — 0.8 kilometre (0.5 mile)*

*End of Lake Minnewanka and
Stewart Canyon*

20   Stewart Canyon

It seems very likely that in preglacial time the Cascade River flowed along more or less the middle of the valley floor southeastward into what is now the Bow River valley. Deposits of glacial debris and various meltwater adjustments have caused the postglacial Cascade River to swing eastward a few kilometres above Lake Minnewanka, enter a steep canyon area, and discharge finally into Lake Minnewanka through the now flooded Stewart Canyon.

A short walk from the end of the car road along the end of Lake Minnewanka, where limestones containing an abundance of fossils are exposed here and there, will take you to a footbridge over Stewart Canyon. This very steep walled canyon has been flooded to a depth of several metres by the damming of the outlet of Lake Minnewanka in very recent times, thus making a steep-shored, narrow waterway extending back into the country for more than a thousand metres.

Looking northward along the canyon, the rocks are seen to dip quite steeply to the left or west, and the original canyon was cut more or less down the dip of the rocks themselves.

*Road junction to Stop 21 —
1.6 kilometres (1.0 mile)*

21   Viewpoint, Southeast End of Lake Minnewanka

From the junction, the road runs along the top of a dam that has lifted the level of Lake Minnewanka some 20 metres (65 feet), in order to make a reservoir for hydro-electric power generated near Stop No. 5 beside the Trans-Canada Highway. This has had the effect of beheading the Cascade River, which used to drain Lake Minnewanka down the steep valley just below the road junction and then into the Bow River. The water now flows through a system of canals and lakes just below and to your right as you face Lake Minnewanka, then into flumes and through the power-house. It is interesting to note that in the 40 years or so since the lake

Opposite: Cascade River used to enter Lake Minnewanka through a canyon cut into sloping layers of limestone, with one bank (at right) sloping gently down the dip of the rocks, and the other bank (left) much steeper because of the overhang. When a dam raised the lake, flooding the canyon, this inlet formed.

Right: The waters of Lake Minnewanka shine in the early morning sun, with the bulk of Mount Inglismaldie looming beyond. The lake and the valley leading into it once provided the Indians with an access route into the mountains.

Below: Lake Minnewanka's trough cuts squarely across the mountain structures a few kilometres east of Banff. The rolling foothills make the horizon in the bottom of the trough, framed by the upturned edges of the folded limestone and shale.

was dammed and the level raised, new beaches have been made, new cliffs have been cut, remnants of the old flooded forests virtually removed, and a complete new set of lake features produced.

Visitors to Lake Minnewanka in the early part of the century used to travel by boat up to the end of the lake and then through a narrow channel into another lake. The raising of the surface of Lake Minnewanka has joined the two lakes and obliterated all trace of the intervening channels.

A study of Lake Minnewanka and the valley that it occupies reveals still more of the peculiar drainage history of the area in and about Banff. If you travel to the eastern end of the lake, you can see very clearly that its valley continues with a very flat floor eastward beyond the mountains to the foothills. At one stage a major river system must surely have flowed the length of what is now the Lake Minnewanka valley and out onto the plains. A full description of the drainage changes is given on pages 57 to 64.

The trip down the length of Lake Minnewanka by boat—or along one of the trails on either side—shows many beautiful views, for the valley in which the lake lies crosses the structure of the mountains exposing their internal features. Great sweeping *folds* and *faults* that displace the rock units many hundreds of metres and great limestone cliffs are visible.

Hoodoos of spectacular size are developed in coarse gravels on the south side of the lake near its eastern end in a tributary brook valley. In the early part of the century, pleasure boats used to bring tourists to this area, but now it is rarely visited.

From this viewpoint on the dam, you can see the eastern side of Cascade Mountain with its flank incised by a row of *cirques*—bowllike depressions made by residual glaciers high up on the mountainside. The upper part of the mountain is cut mostly into limestones of Palaeozoic age whereas the wooded lower slopes are for the most part underlain by dark shaly rocks of Cretaceous age. The Cretaceous rocks below the mountain are exposed in the old outlet of Lake Minnewanka below the dam.

The rocks of the Palliser Range, and the Fairholme Range on the opposite (south) side of Lake Minnewanka, show complicated structures developed in folded rocks of the Palliser, Banff, and Rundle formations. One nicely shown *anticline* or upfold is visible in the first high hill to the right of the inlet of Cascade River. To the right of Lake Minnewanka, as you look northeast along this arm, the great cliffs of Palliser limestone on the northern slope of Inglismaldie make a conspicuous feature of the landscape.

Right: Here, near the eastern end of Lake Minnewanka, is one of the huge boulders—this one with trees growing on its top—that are sometimes left perched on hoodoos, as such pillars of eroded glacial material are called.

Below: The boulder on the hoodoo column at the left of the picture overlooks more hoodoos and Lake Minnewanka below them. The body of water beyond the narrows was a separate lake before a dam raised the level of the water.

These steep cliffs to the north of Lake Minnewanka show complicated folding.

Straight down the lake, the ridge at the far end of the view is a great dip slope on and near the flank of an anticline. The massive grey limestone formations make great sweeping curves in the hillsides, with brown streaks of Banff shale angling down and to the right from the left end of the crest.

Lake Minnewanka and the valley leading into it from each end once provided the Indians with an access route into the mountains, and it is odd to stand on this viewpoint now and think that their trails and campsites lie 15 or 20 metres below the surface of this great lake. A little farther on, a plaque recalls the exploits of the Palliser expedition of 1857-60 in this area. Between the dam and Stop No. 22, you will see the canals leading the water out of Lake Minnewanka into Two-Jack Lake and beyond—the Two-Jack Lake campsite—and the beginning of the flumes to take the water over the cliffs into the powerhouse below.

To Stop 22—4.2 kilometres (2.6 miles)

22 Roadside Viewpoint, Just Past Bridge

From here you can look down into the valley of the Bow River, this time in a westerly and southerly direction. Northwest of you the bulk of Cascade Mountain shows the beautiful downfold or *syncline* structure and the massive Palliser limestone cliffs, notched here and there by deep gullies. Below the grey limestones, the dark Cretaceous rocks just show above the wooded slopes to the right. Above the grey

This is another example of the way the rocks of the Palliser Range have been thrown up into great synclines, or downfolds, and anticlines, or upfolds. Scree slopes lie at the bottom of the cliff.

Palliser limestone cliffs are the brown Banff shales that make the middle slopes of the mountain, of more gentle contour, leading to the rugged Rundle limestone in the top cliffs. Sticking up beyond and a little to the west is Mount Norquay with its lower grassed shoulders showing green, and, farther back, other jagged peaks of the Sawback Range.

Straight west, through the gap made by the valley of the Bow River, stands Mount Bourgeau. Other mountains in the distance lead to the right or north to where the view is cut off by Mount Norquay itself. The lump of Tunnel Mountain lies below the end of Mount Rundle, separated from it by the water gap made by the Bow River.

The great mass of glacial debris and glacial outwash filling the whole valley is visible in cuts and banks, appearing as light patches in the wooded valley just below and extending to the mountains on all sides. Immediately below this spot is a small plant for generating power from Lake Minnewanka's water. Beyond it to the right, steep banks of pale yellowish glacial gravels show the beginnings of *hoodoo*-like structures in several places.

This viewpoint presents you with one more aspect of the great Palliser limestone — Banff shale — Rundle limestone sandwich to be seen (from bottom to top) in Mount Rundle, with older rocks being exposed here and there in the wooded slopes below. The edge of the Rundle Range stretches off to the south with knobs and irregular peaks sticking out here and there, looking rather like the edge of a notched board.

Viewpoint to junction with Trans-Canada Highway — 2.6 kilometres (1.6 miles)

From Lake Minnewanka junction along Trans-Canada Highway southward to Tunnel Mountain road junction — 0.56 kilometre (0.35 mile)

Trans-Canada Highway junction to hoodoo turnoff — 2.4 kilometres (1.5 miles)

23   Hoodoo Viewpoint

The road to the hoodoos area follows close to the edge of a steep bank of partly consolidated glacial debris, spread out over the valley floor by meltwaters from retreating glaciers in the fairly recent geological past. At present, the Bow River is cutting sharply into these sands and gravels, exposing them to rainwash, meltwater from snow, and other agents of erosion. In some places these processes have left behind tall pillars of the sands and gravels as erosional remnants. Generally, these structures must have a capping of a large boulder or a horizontal rock layer of some kind to be called *hoodoos,* but in the Banff area the pillars themselves without caps are called that. They occur in several places up and down the Bow River valley and the valley of the Cascade River near here.

From this viewpoint, a look to the

113

southwest along the Bow River shows very well the sharply marked water gap between the toe of Mount Rundle on the south and Tunnel Mountain, its continuation to the north. Beyond the water gap, cut by the Bow River and its ancestors, the wooded slopes of Sulphur Mountain rise to the limestone crest in a series of irregular slopes. Near at hand, the mighty Palliser limestone cliffs near the bottom of Mount Rundle extend off to the east and southeast. Below these, in the woods, occasional outcrops of rocks of Lower Palaeozoic age are seen: above, the gentler slopes are made on the brownish weathering Banff shale. The very crest of Mount Rundle is made of the Rundle limestone and from here it looks like a capping along the top. The slopes seen from here on the northeastern and eastern sides of Mount Rundle are irregular because the rocks dip away from you to the westward, and you are looking at the broken edges of the dipping rock formations. This kind of slope contrasts sharply with the southwestern side of Mount Rundle, which follows the limestone bedding surfaces in great smooth dip slopes.

Opposite: The Hoodoos, about three kilometres east of Banff, are composed of yellowish mud, sand and scattered boulders. Behind them can be seen the great Palliser cliffs of the lower slopes of Mount Rundle.

Below here the Bow River moves moodily on its way to the distant ocean, carrying its load of suspended and dissolved sedimentary materials. Here and there it forms islands where part of its load is temporarily deposited

Hoodoos to Tunnel Mountain road junction in cottage area—
2.1 kilometres (1.3 miles)

Road junction along the Tunnel Mountain road to Stop 24—
0.8 kilometre (0.5 mile)

24 Roadside Stop, Viewpoint on Rocky Point, Tunnel Mountain Road

The rocky point here, partly obscured by trees, provides a view of the Bow River valley and the mountains to the north. Cascade Mountain and a foothill of Mount Norquay, opposite and to the north, show the great strut of the Palliser limestone layers making the great cliffs on so many of the Rocky Mountains. High up in Cascade Mountain the Rundle limestone caps the very peaks, with the brownish weathering Banff shale making softer slopes in between. The rocks immediately behind you and in the rest of Tunnel Mountain are largely made of the same Palliser limestone.

Mount Norquay, opposite, shows the green smooth slopes of the areas

In the foreground are the rushing white waters of the Bow River above Bow Falls, with the great wall of Sulphur Mountain and the Goat Range on the skyline. The abrupt cross valley in the left background is where the Spray River cuts across the limestone formations.

cleared for winter skiing, with cliffs of limestone above. Away to the left or west, horizontally layered Pilot Mountain shows beyond the bend of the Bow River valley. Through a gap in the mountains to the left of Pilot Mountain, you can see westward way beyond to the many peaks near the Continental Divide. Nearer at hand, the wooded slopes of Sulphur Mountain show again outcropping struts of the Palliser limestone in its northern end. To the east, or right as you face outward from the viewpoint, the gap of the valley of Lake Minnewanka is backed by a great wall of rocks. Still farther to the right are Mount Inglismaldie and Mount Girouard.

To Stop 25—2.4 kilometres (1.5 miles)

25 Bow Falls Viewpoint

From the parking area and the foot trails that lead from it down over the point of land, and again from the roadside downhill toward Banff, you can look into the canyon of the Bow River, here floored with a thin sheet of rushing water, which ends in Bow Falls and the calm river below. This section of the Bow River is located more or less along the contact between rocks of the Spray River Formation of Triassic age on the far side, and rocks of the Rocky Mountain Formation on the near side. The Rocky Mountain Formation overlies the Rundle limestone of Mississippian age and is thought to be possibly of Pennsylvanian age. The next several hundred metres or so of road downhill from this viewpoint are marked by the slabby bedding planes of sandy dolomites of this rock group and those just below it. Many of the surfaces of the beds or layers have peculiar patterns on them, which indicate a general shallow-water origin. From many places along the river bank, the *strike* or trend of the rock units is clearly visible on the river bottom through the moving water. You may notice also how the bank you are standing on slopes with the beds, but the far bank is much steeper and is undercut in some places as the river follows down the dip of the overhanging formations.

To the north is Mount Norquay with the green patches of the ski slopes showing, and Mount Brewster beyond with a clear westward dip in the massive limestone units, all part of the same Palliser-Banff-Rundle sandwich seen in so many of the peaks in this area and exemplified so clearly in Mount Rundle. Away to the northwest, Pilot Mountain shows its strongly marked horizontal layering. Nearer and westward, Sulphur Mountain's wooded slopes lead upward to its limestone crest.

As you look southeastward, straight along the Bow River beyond the falls and up the valley of the Spray River, you can see clearly the water gap that the Spray River makes as it cuts across the trend of the ridges called Sulphur Mountain on this side and Goat Range beyond.

117

Roadlog III
Trans-Canada Highway from Banff Cloverleaf (Eastern) to Eisenhower Junction

Banff cloverleaf (eastern) and Stop 7 to overpass and Banff cloverleaf (western) — 4.3 kilometres (2.7 miles)

Western Banff cloverleaf to Vermilion Lakes viewpoint — 0.16 kilometre (0.1 mile)

26 Viewpoint, Vermilion Lakes

Directly below this viewpoint lie the Vermilion Lakes, made of Bow River water backed up on the valley flat. Their principal function seems to be to reflect the beauties of Mount Rundle opposite. On calm days it makes a very beautiful scene indeed, particularly from the lower road.

A closer look at the western side of Mount Rundle shows the great grey dip slopes of the Rundle limestone of Mississippian age. You can follow the Rundle Range off to the south and see that this capping limestone extends along the crest for quite a distance, but then is gradually replaced by the underlying Banff shales; these you can see under the break of the lip on the north shoulder of the peak of Rundle itself. The Banff shale weathers

rather more easily than the limestone and so tends to make softer rounded slopes of brownish *scree*. A great vertical cliff of Palliser limestone of Devonian age shows below the Banff shale. Tunnel Mountain, lying well below Mount Rundle, is clearly seen to be the continuation of the same rock layers, but it is cut off by the water gap made by the Bow River in its very peculiar course near Banff.

Directly opposite this viewpoint, the green slopes with occasional struts of grey limestone mark the end of Sulphur Mountain. Beyond, the Sundance Range shows brownish peaks and slopes on top with carpeted woods below. To the far right, the cake-shaped mountain showing horizontal layering on top is Mount Bourgeau. Right back of you is Mount Norquay and its subsidiary spurs. The limestone cut, down the road, contrasts with the big cut in glacial debris right next to this stop.

To the left is Mount Inglismaldie, far to the east, the farthest left of a group of fairly high mountains which show some snow all year round. Next to Inglismaldie, a little higher and to the right, is Mount Girouard, followed by a long brownish ridge and then Mount Peechee in irregular grey limestone with a back part clearly showing horizontal layering. These three peaks are just a little under 3,000 metres (or approximately 10,000 feet) high.

The buildings of the Cave and Basin hot springs area can be seen at the foot of Sulphur Mountain. The main strut in Sulphur Mountain is the Palliser limestone with the Banff shale in the wooded area above. The Rundle limestone formation makes a conspicuous grey rib along the right or western slope as seen from here.

To Stop 27—1.6 kilometre (1.0 mile)

27 *Upper Vermilion Lake Viewpoint*

Held by a retaining wall of grey limestone boulders and backed by a cliff of grey limestone, this stop furnishes a view out over the valley floor of the Bow River. The backed-up water of the Bow River makes the Vermilion Lakes, the upper one just to the right and below you. The beautiful sloping peak of Mount Rundle is prominent to the southeast. The great dip slope of the Rundle limestone of Mississippian age makes the smooth western slope of the mountain, contrasting with the broken appearance of the eastern side where, below the Rundle cap rock, lie the gentle brownish slopes made by the Banff shale and the grey limestone cliff of the Palliser limestone of Devonian age below that again.

On many days Mount Rundle has a peculiar little cloud over its peak. This is often made by the movement of the air over its slope. As the air, moving generally eastward, travels up the western slope of the mountain, it rises into a region of lower pressure and lower temperature. If the conditions of humidity and temperature are just right, the water vapour in the air will pass the critical point and condense, thus making a cloud. This is most often seen in the morning and evening and is sometimes very dramatic.

This viewpoint is more or less opposite the end of the valley of Sundance Creek, a very small brook occupying a very large rounded valley. A few kilometres to the south, the Spray River (a much larger stream) occupies the same valley, but it suddenly shifts its course to cut across the ridge made by Sulphur Mountain and its continuation southward, the Goat Range, to flow on in the next adjacent valley. Thus, it seems that Sundance Creek occupies the valley cut by a much larger river in earlier times, but whose waters are now pirated or stolen from it by the drainage system in the adjacent valley. This is but a tiny episode in the story of very complicated drainage changes that have affected the Banff area. These changes are discussed more fully on pages 57 to 64.

The southern end of the Sawback Range in the valley of Forty Mile Creek provides this spectacular view of rocks standing on edge, about seven kilometres west of Banff. The sharp peak in the centre is Mount Louis.

The wide sweeping lines of the Sundance Creek valley are bounded by the end of Sulphur Mountain on the left and Sundance Range on the right. Far to the east, down the Bow River valley and beyond, you can just see the tip of Mount Inglismaldie. Westward, horizontally layered rocks make several peaks including Mount Bourgeau on the left, its flat cakelike peak being the back of a large *cirque*.

To stop 28 — 2.6 kilometres (1.6 miles)

28 Intersection of Trans-Canada Highway and Route 1A, Railway Overpass and Bow River Bridge

The Bow River, having flowed generally parallel to the valley systems for many tens of kilometres, suddenly turns eastward across the trend of the mountains for a short distance. This part of the valley, then, and that below it for several kilometres, is marked by the exposed ends of the long windrowlike mountain ranges that extend generally northwest-southeast in this part of Banff National Park. The first ridges that the Bow cuts through in its eastward course include the vertical ribs of the Sawback Range and its extension to the south in the Sundance Range.

120

Right back of this area, for example, the vertical ribs of Mount Edith (Palliser limestone) are visible up a valley to the north, with the grey limestone of Mount Norquay to the northeast. Dark shaly rocks of Triassic age in the lowermost slopes of Mount Norquay extend all the way down to the highway, where they make the black and dark grey outcrops there.

The distant peaks just visible through the trees to the east along the road are Inglismaldie, Girouard, and Peechee; they lie some 15 kilometres eastward and southward of the Lake Minnewanka valley. The view of the grey limestone slopes of Mount Rundle is cut off by the wooded slopes of Sulphur Mountain, gashed by a road zig-zagging up to the experimental station near the top at the end of a long row of grey limestone peaks. The Sundance Range, to the right across the large open wooded valley, shows smooth, brownish slopes on top. Westward up the river valley from here, the mountains show more of a horizontal layering and are cut very largely in rocks that are considerably older than those of the mountain peaks nearby and to the east. They lie generally in the Main Ranges of the Rocky Mountain System. Above and below the bridge an interesting variety of currents in the Bow River makes intricate patterns in the water.

To Stop 29 — 3.8 kilometres (2.4 miles)

29 Roadside Stop at Curve and Outcrop, 0.6 kilometre (0.4 mile) beyond Sunshine Road Intersection

Magnificent slabs of limestone standing on edge mark the southern end of the Sawback Range, with more jagged points standing up farther back along the crest. To the east, Sulphur Mountain's wooded slope is scarred by the zigzag road that leads to the experimental station on its limestone crest. Above and beyond the left (or north) end of the ridge, the peaks of Mount Rundle show their grey limestone. Nineteen kilometres away to the northwest, Mount Eisenhower and the horseshoe extension of its rock formations to the east loom large.

At this place the Bow River swings abruptly from its southeasterly trend, parallel to the mountain ranges, which it has followed for many tens of kilometres, to a northeasterly course that exposes the truncated ends of the mountain ranges for a few kilometres. In this immediate area the valley flat of the Bow River is underlain by thick sands and gravels, probably mostly glacial outwash. Numerous small pockets have been left in this gravelly plain by the irregularities of river erosion and perhaps the original glacial deposition, so that

121

The east side of the Sawback Range provides many examples of mountains formed of nearly vertical rocks.

numerous small ponds and backwaters are to be seen in it.

Northwestward from here, the layer-cake top of Pilot Mountain makes a conspicuous landmark—in fact, it got its name because it is visible for many kilometres up and down the Bow River valley and was used for navigation by pioneer travellers. Nearer than the peak of Pilot Mountain and to the left (looking north), you can see a great mass of east-dipping limestone with layer-cake horizontal bedding behind part of Mount Bourgeau.

To Stop 30 — 4.3 kilometres (2.7 miles)

30 Roadside Stop at Widened Section Beside Bow River

The Bow River moves steadily across the front of this viewpoint as you look across the valley toward the Sawback Range. You will begin to realize what enormous forces there were within the earth's crust when you think that the rocks now standing almost on edge in the Sawback Range once accumulated as flat horizontal layers beneath an ancient sea. Since these beds were thrust up on edge, erosion has produced a complex array of peaks and slopes by cutting into the rock layers, sometimes parallel to the layering, sometimes at a gentle angle across it, and sometimes directly across it. In places, you can see a conspicuous layering in the rocks reflected in a clearly marked banding in the pattern of vegetation on the mountain slopes. This is because different rock layers give slightly different growing conditions, making vegetation much more successful in some places than in others. The open grassy meadows that show light green among the dark forests and grey limestones are where heavy snows have accumulated and subsequent snowslides have cleared out the larger trees, or where moisture conditions do not allow trees to grow at all.

An unusual feature visible from here is the Hole in the Wall, a large gap in the limestone just to the right of a spot directly under the first knob at the south end of the Sawback Range. This hole was probably eroded out of the limestone by glacial meltwater some time ago when glaciers were far larger and more widespread than now.

Off to the north, the edges of the upturned rock units form the jagged peaks and chevron slopes that have given the name to this mountain group. The high end of the near mountains in this range is Mount Ishbel. Beyond it you can see the continuation of the Sawbacks with their typical structure. The Sawback Range is continued to the south of the Bow River valley in the Sundance Range, where the same kind of structures may be seen from points opposite that range in the Brewster Creek valley. Directly beyond and above the Trans-Canada Highway to the north, a distinct westerly dip is clearly visible in the rocks that lie generally to the east of Mount Eisenhower.

To Stop 31 — 3.7 kilometres
(2.3 miles)

31   Roadside Stop Beside Abandoned Service Road to East

The superb layer-cake top of Pilot Mountain looms above the highway in this section. In the early part of the summer, the snow on this high peak marks the bedding in the Rundle limestone where erosion has carved ledges and depressions. Below that, the brown shoulders made by the Banff Formation lie above high cliffs of Palliser limestone. This again is the same

The Hole in the Wall (lower centre) is a solution cavity cut into the limestones of the Sawback Range.

Palliser-Banff-Rundle sandwich found in a great many of the peaks of the eastern Rocky Mountains up and down the length of the national parks.

This viewpoint provides an ideal spot to contrast the *dogtooth mountains* of the Sawback Range, carved on nearly vertical rock layers, with *layer-cake mountains* carved into rock layers that are nearly horizontal.

From here, straight up the road, you can see the general structure of Mount Eisenhower and the peaks to the immediate east. The snowy peaks in the middle of the complex lie back of Mount Eisenhower as you see it from the highway directly opposite it. To the right of this area the dip of the rocks down and to the left or west is clearly visible. To the left of the snowy peaks, Mount Eisenhower itself sticks up above the tree line and you can see that the rock units there, though nearly horizontal, do have a very gentle dip to the east, so that the whole complex is part of a downfold or *syncline.* Unseen by most travellers in this area are two beautiful lakes behind Mount Eisenhower, immediately below the steep cliffs that you see from here under the snowy peaks. The larger one, Rockbound Lake, lies at the back, encircled in cliffs in the centre of the syncline. The smaller one, fed by its outlet, lies far below in wooded seclusion.

To Stop 32 — 2.9 kilometres (1.8 miles)

32   Mount Eisenhower Viewpoint

This viewpoint and parking area beside the Bow River is marked by a large boulder of dark *argillite* set in a mosaic of flagstones from the Spray River quarry near Banff (see Stop No. 14). From this viewpoint a great deal of the geology and scenery of the lower Bow River valley is visible. To the northwest, the view of the southeastern end of Mount Eisenhower and Helena Ridge to the right show very clearly the synclinal structure of the area, with easterly dips in Mount Eisenhower and westerly dips in Helena Ridge. In the centre part of the downfold you may be able to see the line of steep cliffs that lies at the back of Rockbound Lake, not visible from anywhere along the highway. From here also you can look at the *fault* along which the whole mass of Mount Eisenhower and the adjacent hills has slid up over the rocks to the east. Its *trace,* or line of dislocation, lies in the woods under the rocky ramparts of Mount Eisenhower and runs gently up the slope under the low grassy peak between the

wooded point to the right and the rocky ones to the left. On this great break that extends for scores of kilometres to the north and many kilometres to the south, a huge mass of flat-lying or gently dipping rocks has been thrust up to the east over younger rocks. It is this same fault system that is visible in Jasper National Park between Pyramid Mountain on the west and the Palisade on the east.

The great bulk of Mount Temple is a little to the left of Mount Eisenhower as you look at it up the river. Southward, down the river valley, you can see the layered peak of Pilot Mountain, but the horizontal layering in the mountain is not as conspicuous from here as it is farther to the south because of this end view.

Across the valley to the east, the distinct chevrons of the Sawback Range, with the inverted *V*'s of Mount Ishbel opposite, loom over the rounded hills with their woods and open meadows. The peaks of the Sawbacks are all in rocks of Mississippian and Devonian age, whereas the rounded hills and meadows are developed on later Palaeozoic and Mesozoic rocks. These all lie below the southward extension of the Castle Mountain *thrust* or fault surface mentioned earlier. The limestone in the cliffs and the dark green hill opposite belong to the Palaeozoic groups. It is interesting to note a great hole in

Above: Mount Ishbel, with its head in the clouds, rises 2,877 metres (9,440 feet) above sea level. *Below:* In this closer view of Mount Ishbel, you can see where a great mass of limestone has pulled away from the nearly vertical wall, cascaded downward, and formed a cone-shaped scree slope.

one of the dip slopes in the limestones below and a little to the left of the peak of Mount Ishbel. Jointing in the massive limestones is in two directions, which now are more or less diagonal up and down the slopes of the limestone beds. The hole was made when a large mass of limestone became detached, then slid diagonally down and to the right along one of the joint surfaces. The waste from this slide has added an enormous bulk of broken rock to the scree slope below.

You may note the lines of vegetation following the rock units along the flank of the Sawback Mountains, especially to the south or right as you face across the valley. These are formed simply by the differing success of vegetation in different rock units, probably controlled mostly by the presence or absence of moisture and footing.

Immediately below the viewpoint, the Bow River is busily building and destroying islands of sand and gravel, with the tall straight dark spruce trees standing as mute witnesses of these activities on the valley flat just beyond.

The wall around the viewpoint is built of split boulders of quartzites, Precambrian and lower Cambrian in age. If you look closely at the split surfaces of these, you will see lots of pale flakes which have lifted a little but have not quite come off during the breaking process; pink, grey, and brown are the most common colours, with some a pale green. Some of these quartzites are made of very fine sand, while others show strings of pebbles in them, and they may or may not have layering.

Among the quartzite boulders are some grey limestone boulders which tend to flake a little but weather white and are not as hard as the quartzite masses. From the composition of the rocks in this wall and a knowledge of the occurrence of rocks up and down the valley, you can tell that this material has been hauled from west of here because that is where these rocks outcrop.

To Stop 33 — 6.7 kilometres (4.2 miles)

33 Stop Beside Bow River Bend

The towers of middle Cambrian limestone in Mount Eisenhower clearly show a dip down and to the right, then a flattening and reversal of dip down to the left in Helena Ridge farther to the right or east. This enormous *synclinal mass* (downfold) of rocks has been thrust up over a *fault surface* onto younger rocks. The fault surface itself lies under the grassy round knob on the skyline, and its *trace* or line of dislocation passes down through the wooded slopes well beneath Mount Eisenhower. You can clearly see how different the rocks are just

Mount Eisenhower, with a height of 2,752 metres (9,030 feet) above sea level, dominates the scene for many kilometres along the Bow River valley and here presents a view of great beauty.

above the fault trace, where old quartzites prevail, and just below it, where there are younger limestones.

Across the valley the chevron ridges of the Sawback Range form all the skyline to the southeast. Mount Ishbel pokes up its *V*-shaped summit on the left, high over the highest, green-meadowed foreground ridges. Northward, the mass of the Central Ranges of the Rockies culminates in the snowy horizontal-layered Mount Temple at 3,549 metres (11,636 feet) above sea level. You can see that the nearer peaks are fronted all along by *cirque* basins (bowl-shaped depressions carved by local glaciers) that widen out just above the present timber line.

Nearby, the Bow River busily erodes and deposits sands and gravels, building islands and sand bars at one place and tearing them away at another. Here, the channel splits and joins around a large wooded island.

To Stop 34 — 2.6 kilometres (1.6 miles)

34 Eisenhower Junction

To the south and southeast, the Sawback Range points sharp edges to the sky. Northeastward, more or less across the Bow River valley, Mount Eisenhower presents its full spread of towers and terraces. From here, you are looking almost diagonally at the edges of rock beds or layers that are dipping nearly horizontally, although from a little farther to the south you can see that they have a dip of a few degrees away from you or to the east. Copper Mountain sticks up above the woods to the south (to the right of the road if you stand with your back to Mount Eisenhower). You can also see the bulk of Storm Mountain with its snowy cap just to the right of the highest peak and a deep nick in the long right-hand slope. This great mass is formed almost entirely of quartzite of Lower Cambrian and Precambrian age.

To the right of Storm Mountain as you look at it from here, Boom Mountain with its square top is conspicuous. Boom Lake lies under its right flank. A jagged skyline leads to the right toward the high peaks of Moraine Lake. The nearer mountains in this panorama are *cirque*-pitted along the front. Beyond them lies the snowy top of Mount Temple. From the north side of the cloverleaf at Eisenhower Junction, you can see the white splash of icefields and glaciers between the Waputik Range and the crest of the Continental Divide some 56 kilometres to the northwest, and beyond the turn of the Trans-Canada Highway from the Bow River valley into Kicking Horse Pass. From the north side of the cloverleaf, too, you can see an abandoned channel of the Bow River close to the highway with a little bit of water still in it.

Roadlog IV
Eisenhower Junction to Vermilion Pass and Kootenay National Park

*Eisenhower Junction to Stop 35 —
5.4 kilometres (3.4 miles)*

35 Storm Mountain Viewpoint Opposite Cabins

The bend in the road here, high on the shoulder of the hill, provides excellent views out over the valley of Altrude Creek and both eastward to the Bow River valley and westward toward Kootenay National Park. Directly opposite, the great bulk of Storm Mountain shows deep bowl-shaped *cirques* cut into Precambrian and Lower Cambrian quartzites on its east face. Away to the right or west, framed in the *V* gap, a part of the grey steep Rock Wall shows one of the principal scenic features of Kootenay National Park. Some high glaciers are just visible on the left, and snowfields can be seen lower to the right. On the right side of the valley, looking west, a sharply truncated spur marks the spot where Tokumm Creek comes in from the

---

Opposite: Not many visitors to Banff National Park see this lovely lake just behind Mount Eisenhower. It is seen here from the southeastern shoulder of the mountain, just below the upper tower.

northwest to join the southwest-flowing Vermilion River above a great rock wall cut into Cambrian limestones above and quartzites below. Nearer, the horizontally layered Mount Whymper shows a pointed peak.

Still farther to the right, now west-northwest from where you are standing, Boom Mountain shows a gentle back slope toward the west with a steep eastern side, and a glimpse of the glaciers that lie at the head of Boom Lake hidden in the valley to the right. Eastward, the great wall of Mount Eisenhower with its vertical turrets and horizontal layering contrasts with the serrate Sawback Range in the distance to the right or southeast. The bulk of Mount Eisenhower and most of Helena Ridge immediately behind it belong to a huge mass of rocks thrust up, along a *fault,* over the rocks that lie to the east. From this viewpoint the trace or line of the fault lies just to the right of three grassy knobs at the right of Eisenhower's towers and just below a distant *V*-shaped peak poking up behind them. From that point, the trace follows more or less straight down the slope, then curves gently to the left underneath Eisenhower itself. Some of Copper Mountain's bare top pokes out over the woods to the south.

For those who are following this guidebook and are driving now toward Eisenhower Junction, watch carefully as you come down from this viewpoint to the junction on the floor of the Bow River valley for the magnificent views of Mount Eisenhower. For those who are continuing into Kootenay Park and will return later, keep this in mind for this is one of the splendid views in the Canadian Rockies. Little wonder that the early settlers called this great mountain Castle Mountain.

To Stop 36 — 2.9 kilometres (1.8 miles)

36 Vista Lake Viewpoint

Away to the east down the valley of Altrude Creek, the wall of Mount Eisenhower leading to Protection Mountain to the left is visible against the background of the Sawback Range to the southeast. The *V*-shaped peak of Mount Ishbel in the Sawbacks shows a great hole, which looks like a light window in the limestone slopes. The hole was left when a great mass of rocks broke out and cascaded down to the scree slopes below.

Westward and across the road, the great walls of Mount Whymper dominate the scene with the marks of fresh rockfalls clearly shown as light streaks and scars. A brown-orange spur of Boom Mountain looms to the right. Across the valley, Storm Mountain shows dipping Precambrian and Lower Cambrian quartzite series in its reddish brown slopes. High and to the right of Storm Mountain is Stanley Peak with its snowy top with glaciers here and there. The symmetrical peak of Mount Vermilion beyond shows more gentle slopes to the south of that group. Straight down the road, the distant Rock Wall—well inside Kootenay National Park—shows one high glacier and one low one, quite clear from here. Vista Lake lies on the valley bottom far below this viewpoint in its dark sylvan setting of forest and burned forest. Opposite and lower down, remnants of a moraine loop along the base of Storm Mountain, showing that the glaciers were once here.

To Stop 37 — 1.9 kilometres (1.2 miles)

37 Western Boundary Banff National Park and Continental Divide

The western Banff National Park boundary is the eastern boundary of Kootenay National Park, both following the Continental Divide in an irregular serpentine course for many kilometres here near Vermilion Pass. If you stop at the sign showing the Continental Divide, you will be able to look up the hills on both sides of the road and see the boundary as cleared lines through the woods, going up the flanks of Boom Mountain to the northwest

Above: A great mass of Lower Cambrian and Precambrian quartzite forms Storm Mountain, which rises to 3,161 metres (10,372 feet). Its eastern slope is in Banff National Park and its western slope in Kootenay National Park. *Below:* Boom Lake is seen with Quadra Mountain (centre) and Bident Mountain (right).

and a subsidiary spur of Storm Mountain to the southeast.

The outcrops along the road in Banff National Park just to the northeast of the boundary are grey quartzites of the St. Piran Formation. If you examine the slopes of the rocks and continue them to the southeast in your mind's eye, you can see at once that the mountain there must be made of the same rock formation as is the front of Boom Mountain to the northwest.

When rain falls in this area, or when the snow melts in the springtime, the water in the run-off is split into two drainage systems with very different routes. The water on the east side of the Continental Divide flows eastward through Altrude Creek to join the Bow River near Eisenhower Junction and ultimately the Saskatchewan river system, which carries it into Hudson Bay. On the other side of the divide, the water flows into a small brook that joins the headwaters of the Vermilion River, empties into the Kootenay, then the Columbia, and finally the Pacific Ocean near Portland, Oregon.

Looking westward toward Kootenay National Park, Mount Whymper dominates the scene to the right; and Stanley Peak and adjacent mountains, cut in horizontal rocks and with their snow and glaciers, are predominant to the left. Looking eastward, on the other hand, the ramparts of Mount Eisenhower loom large across the valley of the Bow River, with various ridges of the Sawback Range farther distant to the right.

Roadlog V
Trans-Canada Highway
from Eisenhower Junction
to Lake Louise Junction

Eisenhower Junction (Stop 34) to
Stop 38 — 8.6 kilometres
(5.4 miles)

38 Roadside Stop Just North of
Taylor Creek Crossing

The road is next to the Bow River here, and the view is open. Across the valley loom the towers and battlements of Mount Eisenhower. Rock runnels lead down into the timber from the cliffs above, showing how a steady wastage of the mountain supplies constant streams of rock debris that keep these pathways open. The grey cliffs at the top of the mountain are underlain by more brownish rocks, which rise gradually as you follow them southward to form the southern towers and peaks of Eisenhower itself. The rock layers appear almost horizontal from here, but they actually dip away from you at a very gentle angle, for this is the edge of a syncline or downfold that *plunges* very gently to the north. You may get some idea of this by taking a pile of writing paper and bowing it downward. As you look at the edge, the layers made by the individual sheets seem to be more or less horizontal yet they actually dip away from you.

Nearly opposite this viewpoint is the gash of an erosional valley that separates Eisenhower from another segment of the mountain, Protection Mountain, farther to the north.

Part of the Sawback Range is just visible away in the distance downstream. On the right side of the Bow River valley, Copper Mountain shows a bold front and a more gentle back slope, with the brownish lower front area showing snow patches. Just to the left of Copper Mountain is a glimpse of Pilot Mountain.

The bulk of Storm Mountain lies to the southwest with a very big white snow patch on its right flank. Just peeking from behind it on the left is Mount Ball. Northward up the valley of the Bow River, Mount Richardson's jagged profile shows east-sloping layers in its peak. The squared-off Bow Peak is just visible at the edge of the woods to the northwest.

Right here, the Bow River is in a partly controlled channel with the embankment of the roadway on one side and a man-made bank on the other.

To Stop 39 — 9.9 kilometres
(6.2 miles)

39 Turnout and Picnic Area
North of Moraine Creek Crossing

Northward up the highway the skyline is made of the mountains of

135

the Waputik Range, with Bow Peak to the right. As you swing your view a little to the right, Mount Richardson with its jagged top shows one conspicuous snow band following the gentle eastward dip of the rocks in its peak. Mount Temple's sheer-sided mass is above the wooded bank across the road to the southwest. The mountains showing through the trees are on the other (south) side of the Moraine Lake gap. Straight southeastward along the road, Copper Mountain is farthest left along the bare ridges. Storm Mountain is the high one with the icecap farther to the right or southwest. Across the valley from here, flat-looking beds in the Eisenhower syncline are grey on top and more brownish below, with flat *mesa*-like erosional remnants here and there along the ridge. The ridge of Mount Eisenhower continues from the southern end, more or less continuously northward into the part opposite this, the left or northwest end of which is known as Protection Mountain.

To Stop 40 — 5.1 kilometres (3.2 miles)

40 Junction of Trans-Canada Highway and Route 1A

The main route through Banff National Park used to be along what is now Route 1A, following the northeasterly side of the Bow River valley. The old road is now an alternate route, with different views from those on the main Trans-Canada Highway. The new highway follows the southwesterly side of the Bow River between here and a point about 8 kilometres west of Banff where the two join again.

A most unusual outcrop occurs on the north side of the road along Route 1A about a metre off the Trans-Canada Highway. Folded, bedded rocks here are intersected by a series of joints, which all combine to make the rock break into peculiar sticklike fragments that cover the outcrop and display a most unusual pattern.

To the southwest, Mount Temple thrusts its peak into the sky and shows on its northeastward slope a dazzling white glacier. Farther to the right, assorted peaks with ice and snow occupy the skyline in the general direction of Moraine Lake. Mount Fay shows a patch of snow on its right flank and Quadra Mountain shows one isolated peak, then a long flat but serrated skyline with snow below the serrate shoulders. These are visible just over the woods to the left of Mount Temple. East along Route 1A, the ridge of Cambrian rocks is called Protection Mountain on the left or north end. This same ridge extends with little interruption southward to Mount Eisenhower.

Lake Louise road to Whitehorn Sedan junction — 2.4 kilometres (1.5 miles)

Above: Sedimentary layers criss-crossed by regularly spaced joints make this pattern in a rock outcrop near Lake Louise. *Below:* In the same outcrop area, where the joints are farther apart, these peculiar sticks of rock weather out.

41 Junction of Trans-Canada Highway with Road to Whitehorn Sedan Lift and Ski Area

Northeastward up the valley of the Bow River, the Waputik Range shows jagged peaks beyond the near wooded hill. To the left is a prominent inclined shoulder with a considerable icefield leading to Bath Glacier along its lower slope. Still farther left, the high brownish peak is Mount Bosworth. Below Bosworth and to the left as you look up the main valley, the gap in the mountains is Kicking Horse Pass across the Continental Divide. The Trans-Canada Highway and the main line of the Canadian Pacific Railway both use this route westward.

Directly west or across the valley, the mountains surrounding Lake Louise show numerous patches of ice and snow with beautiful glaciers hanging high on the back of the bowl in which Lake Louise itself lies. Valleys along the west side of the Bow River valley are now more or less *hanging valleys,* that is, they were cut on the flanks of the main valley when it was full of ice so that the bottoms of the valleys on the sides now are considerably above the bottom of the main valley itself. Great banks of outwash all along the west side are being cut into by the rivers and streams there and are visible in highway cuts of the Lake Louise road.

Mount Temple's superb mass stands high above the valley wall showing its dazzling white glacier all the way to the tip. Farther left the partial ring made by Mounts Bident, Quadra, and Fay shows a lovely white necklace of ice and snow.

To western Lake Louise turnoff—
0.5 kilometre (0.3 mile)

Western Lake Louise turnoff to
junction of Trans-Canada and
Banff-Jasper highways—
1.9 kilometres (1.2 miles)

Opposite, above: Lake Louise gleams among the dark woods in the bottom of a tremendous bowl, with soaring glacier-hung mountains beyond. The light patch above the lake is an accumulation of rock debris brought down by glaciers in times past. The distant view of the lake *(below)* is seen from the top of the sedan lift.

Roadlog VI
Lake Louise and Moraine Lake Areas

Trans-Canada Highway to Lake Louise junction, via old southern entrance—0.6 kilometre (0.4 mile); via northern entrance— 1.0 kilometre (0.6 mile)

Lake Louise road junction to Moraine Lake road junction— 1.1 kilometres (0.7 mile)

Moraine Lake road junction to Lake Louise turnoff— 1.1 kilometres (0.7 mile)

Lake Louise turnoff to Lake Louise parking lot—0.9 kilometre (0.55 mile)

42 Northeast End, Lake Louise

From the parking lot, a walk of a few hundred metres will take you to the northeast end of Lake Louise and one of the most beautiful sights in the Canadian Rockies. Great mountains ring the pale green lake, and on calm days the roar of distant waterfalls and the occasional booming of cracking and falling ice supply intriguing sounds to add to the feast for the eyes.

As you look up the lake toward the distant mountains, you will gradually become aware that the rocks dip gently away from where you are standing, down and under the far peaks. At the shoreline to the left and to right, the rocks are Pre-cambrian in age. The big cliffs on the left and the more wooded slopes on the right are of Lower Cambrian age and dip westward underneath the Middle Cambrian rocks, which constitute most of the great wall whose upper part is wreathed in snow and ice. Only the topmost parts of the peaks, including Mount Victoria, reach upward into the layered rocks far enough to include those of Upper Cambrian age.

The depression in which the waters of Lake Louise are impounded was made when the glaciers, now found only as small remnants in sheltered and high places, once supplied enough ice to fill the whole of the valley you are standing in. At the height of glaciation, ice probably moved off the heights and out along the Lake Louise valley to contribute its mass to an enormous glacier moving southeastward down the present Bow River valley. As the climate warmed, however, the main Bow River valley glacier disappeared and the Lake Louise valley glacier gradually shrank. At an intermediate stage the ice was pouring down the Lake Louise valley, but it terminated by melting at about the present position of the end of Lake Louise. This meant that the great mass of rocks and the debris from the mountains above were deposited there in the form of a massive *terminal moraine*.

The route to Moraine Lake passes along the eastern slopes of Mount Temple and provides a view across Moraine Creek and Moraine Lake to the mountains beyond. The sharp central peak is Mount Babel which rises to 3,104 metres (10,185 feet).

When the climate warmed still more, the ice retreated because melting was faster than the addition of snow, and the depression behind the terminal moraine was filled with water to form the ancestral Lake Louise. In the last fifty years, the shrinkage of the glaciers—now retreated well back beyond the water-filled depression—has been measured and is known to be fairly rapid. Lake Agnes, which lies back of the Beehive high up and to the right of Lake Louise as you look at it, and other smaller lakes high up in the mountains, generally lie in *cirques*—peculiar bowl-shaped depressions carved by small glaciers high in the mountains.

Horse and walking trails lead to the area beyond the end of Lake Louise where a great variety of glacial deposits in many forms is to be seen in a spectacular setting of rocks, cliffs, and dazzling ice and snow.

In the midst of the mountains at Lake Louise and again at Moraine Lake, you may note that the colour of the rocks tends to warm browns, reddish browns and purplish browns, instead of the light greys and steely greys characteristic of the mountains in the Banff area and in the northern sections of Banff National Park. This is because the rocks are different. Reddish brown or purplish brown quartzites, sandstones and dolomites of Cambrian and Precambrian age prevail in the Main Ranges of the Rocky Mountains. In the Front Ranges the rocks are more usually light grey limestones and dolomites with intermixed shaly layers of Devonian and Mississippian age.

Junction of the Moraine Lake road and the Lake Louise road to Moraine Lake—12.6 kilometres (7.9 miles)

43 Moraine Lake

Moraine Lake is another of the beautiful gems lying in a valley carved by the glaciers among the great peaks of the Rocky Mountains near the Continental Divide. This area, known commonly as the Valley of the Ten Peaks, is ringed by a series of peaks consisting mostly of grey and brown quartzites and slaty shales of Cambrian age. These are broken by more or less vertical joints or cracks, which have had a considerable effect on the erosion of the mountains because they allow the rock to break away from the main mass along these cracks and thus commonly leave vertical or near-vertical faces. The nearly horizontal stratification or layering in the rocks is clearly visible in almost all the peaks. It seems likely that the depression in which Moraine Lake lies began as a glaciated valley, similar to that of Lake Louise. This was at the time when

The trail westward toward Wenkchemna Peak from Moraine Lake presents this view of the glacier-draped upper slopes of Mount Fay.

the glaciers, now found only as remnants high up in the peaks, contributed to a great mass of ice moving down the valley to join the mighty Bow River valley glacier. As the climate warmed, however, the Bow River valley glacier disappeared and the Moraine Lake valley glacier shrank gradually. It left behind, here and there, extensive *terminal moraines* where melting of the ice freed quantities of boulders and rock debris brought from the mountains behind. It seems possible that the ancestral Moraine Lake was formed in this manner.

There is a debate among geologists, however, as to how the mass of boulders and rock rubble that you can walk over at the lower end of Moraine Lake got there. One idea is that landslides, involving huge masses of rocks from near the Tower of Babel (that larger tower of rock on the left as you look at the mountains) collapsed and produced an enormous flowage of rocks which cut across the end of the lake, raising it considerably and making the present dam. The other theory suggests that a temporary renewal of glacial activity produced a long tongue of ice, which picked up a good deal of landslide debris from the *talus* and rock-waste slopes along the lake and pushed it up into those steep masses.

Right: Some of the blocks of quartzite and slaty quartzite show ripple marks like these. They were made millions of years ago, when what is now rock was still soft silty mud on the bottom of the ocean.

Below: The great mass of rocky rubble that dams the lower end of Moraine Lake is made of these great boulders, whose size may be gauged by the figure in the foreground and the people on the top of the mound of rock rubble.

The pile of rubble that dams Moraine Lake may have come from a landslide or from glacial action, or both.

Moraine Lake back along the road to Stop 44 — 2.2 kilometres (1.4 miles)

If you have time to sit on the top of the hill above Moraine Lake you may find it fun to compare the two bodies of evidence, and no matter which you eventually decide on, you may certainly conclude that it took a tremendous force to build up that great pile of large rocks and small fragments. And yet this force was a mere trifle compared to the enormous thrusts within the earth's crust that must have been necessary to form the mighty mountain peaks—thrusts powerful enough to raise those huge masses of rock from the bottom of the sea where they originated long ago.

44 *Viewpoint Over the Valley of Moraine Creek*

From this perch, high on the valleyside, the spread of several of the ten peaks shows to the south and southwest around the hollow occupied by Moraine Lake. Fan-shaped *scree* slopes made from the wasting rocks above are characteristic. The leftmost, sharp peak is Mount Babel, with the Tower of Babel showing a flat top well below and a hole on its northeast face making a great arch. To the left of Babel, a valley leads to the Consolation Lakes and a jagged spur from Quadra Mountain. Near its top a

A mass of glacial ice occupies a shelf below the sharp edge of Bident Mountain. The *bergschrund*—the great crack made by the pulling away of the glacial ice from the wall at the back—is visible as an irregular black line.

glacier extends in behind Babel to Mount Fay. A great *bergschrund* or crack extends all along the back of the glaciers where the glacial ice has pulled away from the rock wall. Immediately back of it the great mass of Mount Temple thrusts skyward.

The flat rocks of Protection Mountain, across the valley of the Bow River to the east, are dark above and softer brown in slopes to the tree line below. Far below you here on the valley floor, Moraine Creek flows in a flat shallow sheet to where it steepens and gets white again. On quiet days you can hear very distinctly its rushing sound.

On the way back to the Trans-Canada Highway, you may wish to note the steep banks of water-washed glacial debris into which the road is cut in this neighbourhood and again on the way down into the main Bow River valley.

Roadlog VII
Trans-Canada Highway from Junction with Banff-Jasper Highway to Kicking Horse Pass and Yoho National Park

45 Junction, Trans-Canada and Banff-Jasper Highways

An unusual outcrop of slaty shale, folded into great curved slabs as part of a *syncline* or downfold, features the southeastern corner of the cloverleaf area. The rock is cut by joints more or less at right angles to the beds or layers, which makes an interesting pattern sometimes in the way the rock breaks out of the cliffs. If you look carefully along the outcrop up the branch from the Trans-Canada Highway that leads northward to the Banff-Jasper highway, you will see that a little of the bottom of the syncline or downfold is preserved in the upper or farther end of the outcrop. Along the highway to the south for several kilometres the slaty splitting cuts across the layering in the outcrops.

To the northwest of this area the Waputik Mountains are a conspicuous mass, with an icefield showing to the left in the cliffs on the east side of the Continental Divide. West-southwestward toward the Lake Louise area, may be seen the mass of Mount St. Piran and behind it and a little higher, Mount Niblock.

From the west side of the interchange there is an excellent view of glaciers and rocky peaks high above to the southeast side of the Lake Louise valley. The mass of white at the back is on Mount Victoria and the circle of mountains leading to Mount Aberdeen to the left. Away to the left is Mount Temple. All the mountains in these masses and the dark ones to the right are formed in Precambrian and Cambrian rocks.

Intersection of Trans-Canada and Banff-Jasper highways to Stop 46— 2.4 kilometres (1.5 miles)

46 Roadside Stop, 90 Metres South of Railway Overpass

A view up the Bath Creek valley, a little to the right of the highway here, shows the glacier and snowfield on the back of the Waputik Range. To the left is Bath Glacier, backed by walls of Cambrian limestone with last year's snow lying along the base. Meltwater from these icy masses feeds the headwaters of Bath Creek, crossed just a little farther on from here and flowing alongside the road at this stop. Southward, the mass of Mount Niblock has horizontal snow lines marking the trace of the Cambrian beds. Mount St. Piran is lower and to the left and is cut

Very fine-grained slaty rocks occur in roadside exposures at several places between Lake Louise junction and the junction of the Trans-Canada and Banff-Jasper highways. Many of the rocks show a slaty cleavage cutting across the horizontal bedding.

---

mostly in Precambrian and Lower Cambrian quartzites. The same quartzites are visible on the east side of the Lake Louise valley, seen to the left of the wooded slope. Down the road, Protection Mountain shows a rather undistinguished series of slopes of Precambrian and Cambrian rocks. A long line of grey and brown cliffs marks Mount Eisenhower's northward extension and leads to the horizon far to the south. Mount Bosworth, with more or less horizontal layering, sticks up on the right side of the Kicking Horse Pass to the west.

To Stop 47 — 4.0 kilometres (2.5 miles)

47 Viewpoint

To the west, up the hill and above

the road in your view, are the snow- and glacier-covered flanks below the pinnacles of the Cathedral Crags in Yoho National Park. The tip of Mount Bosworth is grey and brown above the trees a little to the right (generally westward). The end of the Waputik Range shows reddish above the trees northwest of this point. Back along the road toward the Bow River valley is Mount Richardson, with strong horizontal layering in its peak and lower down. Far to the left, almost straight north of here, Mount Hector shows nearly vertical cliffs of Cambrian limestone in its peak just above the trees. Southward, a complex of snowy peaks include Niblock, Popes Peak in the centre, and Narao just showing to the right. This great mountain mass, lying generally northwest of the valley of Lake Louise, is cut in rock of Lower and Middle Cambrian age with some Precambrian rock showing below.

Outcrops of ancient quartzites are to be seen here and there along the road; a good chance to see some of them is in the old pit across the road from this viewpoint.

To Stop 48 — 1.0 kilometre (0.6 mile)

48   Boundary Between Yoho and Banff National Parks and Continental Divide

The sign that welcomes you to Yoho National Park (and welcomes you to Banff National Park on the other side) is located exactly on the Continental Divide, that is, the line that divides the area drained into the Pacific Ocean on the west from that drained into the Atlantic Ocean on the east. You may very well ask what it is doing on the side of a hill along which the road is generally inclined. The answer lies in the peculiar slopes here, for they may be inclined this way and that but the water in the bottom of the valley turns to the right or west on one side of the Continental Divide, while on the other it turns left (as you look at it from here).

To the south a mass of limestone, shale, quartzite, and grey cliffs of Precambrian quartzites lying below, forms the great block of mountains between you and the deep gash of the Lake Louise valley. Tiny Ross Lake is out of sight below the lowest rock wall to the right. Westward, the snowy mass of Cathedral Mountain leads right toward the Cathedral Crags. To the right of the valley you are in, the horizontal layering of Mount Bosworth is distinctive. To the east lies Protection Mountain with its rounded and irregularly wooded slopes. Westward along the road, you can see a small part of Mount Field, and right in the notch made by the valley through which the road goes you get a glimpse of the reddish rocks of the distant Van Horne Range.

The old gateway marks the Continental Divide where the highway from Lake Louise to Field crosses the divide. The high mountains in the background are part of the Paget Peak - Mount Bosworth mass.

Yoho-Banff boundary west along Trans-Canada Highway—about 2.7 kilometres (1.7 miles); back along the old highway toward Lake Louise to Great Divide— 6.1 kilometres (3.8 miles)

49 *Great Divide on Old Highway*

A wooden arch built of massive logs marks where the old highway crosses the Continental Divide (here called the Great Divide). At this point the divide is a most interesting one because a single brook comes tumbling down the mountainside from the south, then splits in two on a fan of sands and gravels; one branch shifts left or westward to join the Kicking Horse River and the Pacific coast drainage, while the other branch of the same brook swings to the right or east to join the Bow river system, emptying into Hudson Bay. Imagine now, by just stirring your finger in the water of these two little creeks, you can affect erosion all across the continent in two directions!

To the west is the bulk of Mount Bosworth, mostly brown with some grey streaks and made of Lower and Middle Cambrian rocks. Visible to the south are a few of the peaks of the mass of mountains between the uppermost Kicking Horse region and the gash of the Lake Louise valley. The reddish quartzites of the end of the Waputik Mountains are seen over the trees to the right of Mount Bosworth, that is, almost due north of here. Eastward, across the Bow River valley, Mount Richardson's peak shows cliffs lined with horizontal patches of snow marking the bedding.

To Stop 50 — 3.2 kilometres (2.0 miles)

50 Roadside Stop on Embankment

An embankment across a small valley provides a viewpoint for some of the landmarks in the region. The break through the trees made by the road points at the flat greys and browns of the northward extension at Mount Eisenhower to the southeast. In the other direction it points at the lower slopes of Mount Bosworth. From the gravel bank where the old road was, you can see Bath Glacier to the north with a great rock wall at the back and the end of the Waputik Range to the right. Across the valley, Mount Richardson shows clearly horizontal snow lines that mark its stratification or layers. You can identify Mount Richardson by the big valley that seems to come out of its encircling form. Northward many kilometres, lies the castlelike peak of Mount Hector. An unusual view deep into the back country of Banff National Park may be had from here by looking northeastward to where the valley of the Pipestone River presents a look at the country east of the main Banff-Jasper highway.

The drive from this stop to the junction with the Lake Louise road is mostly through the woods with only occasional glimpses here and there of the scenery opposite.

To junction with Lake Louise road — 4.2 kilometres (2.6 miles)

Roadlog VIII
Route 1A from Junction with Trans-Canada Highway Near Lake Louise to Junction with Trans-Canada Highway About 8 Kilometres West of Banff

(The junction of the Trans-Canada Highway and Route 1A is described as Stop No. 40 on page 136.)

Junction of Trans-Canada Highway and Route 1A to Stop 51—2.7 kilometres (1.7 miles)

51 Roadside Stop on Embankment Beside Railway and Bow River

Looking down the Bow River valley from here, Storm Mountain is high in the skyline with a patch of snow and ice on its shoulder. In the distance beyond and to its left, Mount Ball peeks over it. Directly opposite, Mount Temple rears its spectacular mass skyward in an unusually steep-sided form that it owes to its position between two steep-walled glaciated valleys. The diagonal snow-filled gash is characteristic. To its left and well back, the steep ragged-topped walls of Mount Babel lead downward to the valley of the Consolation Lakes. Quadra's snowy, ragged top wall pokes up to the left, and Mount Fay lies behind Mount Babel to the right of Quadra.

Other peaks with snow and ice to the right are close to the Continental Divide and belong to the Wenkchemna Peaks behind Moraine Lake. The valley next right to Mount Temple is lined with mountainsides that show clearly more or less horizontally banded Precambrian quartzites. Lake Louise valley lies the next to the right, with the Beehive being the horizontally layered rounded mass in the middle of it all. Nearby, big banks of glacial debris, washed out of the ice when it was melting very rapidly, form light yellow, pillary slopes. Just below, the Bow's green waters carry glacial silts on their way to the distant sea.

Typical of the sweeps of rivers is the steep bank you are on here on the outside of the curve and the very low bank on the other side.

To Stop 52—2.7 kilometres (1.7 miles)

52 Roadside Stop in Open Meadows

Mount Temple, a great steep-sided mass of rock with a glacier on its right shoulder as you look at it from here, dominates the landscape across the Bow River valley. From here you look straight up the valley leading to Moraine Lake, just to the left of Mount Temple, to see several of the Ten Peaks and the high mountains leading off to the north or right to the Lake Louise area. The Beehive, a local landmark in the Lake Louise area, shows as a rounded, brownish bulge just to the right, and if you look very carefully you may even see the tiny red spot made by the roof of the tearoom there.

The skyline to the east and southeast, that is the left of the road as you look down the Bow River valley toward Banff, is made of the northward extension of the mass of mountains called Mount Eisenhower on the southern end, and Protection Mountain on the north. The two are separated by a cross valley that is visible from the highway about 8 kilometres south of here, opposite the road leading to the Protection Mountain campground. You may note while driving south from here that straight stretches of road point almost directly at either Copper Mountain's irregular mass that you see framed in the roadway now, or at the horizontally layered Pilot Mountain away to the southeast. Pilot's name comes from the pioneers who used it as a landmark when moving up and down the Bow River valley.

The roundness of the boulders all along the road here is evidence of the fact that they are water-worn, having come from the glacial outwash that once flooded the valley floor.

To Protection Mountain campground— 7.8 kilometres (4.9 miles)

Protection Mountain campground to Stop 53—4.2 kilometres (2.6 miles)

53 Roadside Stop in Open Field Beside Railway, Near Junction with Old Road and Gravel Pit

As you look to the northwest, Mount Temple dominates a long line of mountains stretching along the other side of the Bow River valley. It is readily identifiable by its steep-walled mass and its great elevation, for the top is some 3,548 metres (11,636 feet) above sea level. Southwestward, more or less directly across the road and the Bow River valley, lies Storm Mountain, on the boundary between Banff National Park to the east and Kootenay National Park to the west. It has a smooth right or north slope and a jagged, cliffed, southeast face with a cap of ice and snow to the right of the peak as you look at it from here. To its left you can see Mount Ball, which also lies on the Continental Divide, and to its right the snowy tip of Stanley Peak gives you a glimpse of one of the most beautiful areas in Kootenay National Park.

Eastward, and looming over you, is the great wall of Mount Eisenhower displaying steep cliffs of Cambrian rocks with trees in the lower slopes and meadows above. Rock runnels show where the waste from higher in the mountain tumbles down and keeps the pathways open. As you look at Eisenhower from here, it is difficult to realize that you are looking at the edge of a broad downfold or syncline. In the walls of the gap to the left that separates Mount Eisenhower from its northward extension, you can see the dip of the rocks—away from you here—which gives a hint to the synclinal structure.

Along this section of the road big banks and cuts in glacial outwash—materials that were once caught up and moved by the glaciers in the valley and then washed out by the meltwaters when the glaciers were shrinking—provide the pillary, yellowish sand, gravel, and fine silt.

If you are moving south on this road, note the towers of Mount Eisenhower through the trees to the east as you drive along.

To Stop 54—7.2 kilometres (4.5 miles)

54 Eisenhower Junction Area

It is difficult to keep your gaze from Eisenhower's magnificent yellow-brown limestone cliffs at this spot. Here and there, shaly layers make shelflike breaks in the vertical walls, and you can follow these all along the front of the mountain. Natural alpine meadows occur all along the bottom of the cliffs, and in summer the light green of the grass makes a pleasing contrast with the dark green trees and the brown cliffs above, particularly after a passing shower. Another cliff-making rock layer, obscured at the right, emerges to the left from behind the nearby wooded ridge. If you look closely, you will see a tiny fire lookout tower on the projection of the cliff well to the left.

Westward, the mass of Storm Mountain forms the husky left shoulder of the valley that leads to Kootenay National Park. To its left Mount Ball at 3,314 metres (10,865 feet) above sea level forms a conspicuous hump on the Continental Divide. Storm Mountain is made of Precambrian and Lower Cambrian quartzites, but if you follow the dip of the layers toward Ball Mountain you will be able to see that they dip under its peak, which is topped by younger Cambrian limestones. To the right of the valley leading to Kootenay National Park, great walls of brownish and grey limestone culminate in the peaks of Boom Mountain in the nearer middle of the spread and Mount Whymper, the pointed peak to the left. To the

Opposite: The southeastern tower of Mount Eisenhower is seen here from the shoulder just below it. The size of the circled figure shows what a huge mass of rock this is.

south and southwestward, over the wooded hills, Copper Mountain shows its curving horseshoe shape with snow enclosed in it. To its left, the snowy top of Pilot Mountain peeks from behind the wooded slope.

Silver City plaque — 1.3 kilometres (0.8 mile)

To Stop 55 — 3.0 kilometres (1.9 miles)

55 Roadside Stop in Open Valley in Middle of a Straight Stretch

Across the Bow River valley Copper Mountain's wooded lower slopes give way upwards to its bare peak. To the left of Copper Mountain and due south of this spot, the layered snowy knob of Pilot Mountain continues to be the landmark that it is for many kilometres up and down the Bow River valley. The jagged Sawback Range lies to the southeast, with Mount Ishbel's triangular outline the highest of the peaks. To the right of the river valley as you look northward, Mount Eisenhower's tower stands high on the left of the great synclinal mountain mass. This is a tremendous wad of

---

Opposite: This is the lower falls on Johnston Creek — the first one you come to as you walk upstream from the highway. Visible here are some old solution holes and even some tunnels made by the rushing waters before the stream had cut back so far.

rocks that has been folded into a gentle downfold or *syncline;* if you look closely, you will be able to see that the rocks in the left parts of the towers dip very gently to the right, whereas those in the ridge to the right of the valley behind Mount Eisenhower dip very gently to the left or west. The Castle Mountain *thrust,* along which this great mass of rocks has been moved, lies just to the right and underneath the farthest rocky ridge over the dark woods. Note the natural open meadows among the woods.

To see all the important features at this stop, you may have to move a little bit back and forth along the road on the valley flat. Straight west from here, more or less diagonally across the Bow River valley, is Boom Mountain, a little to the left above the valley in which Boom Lake lies. At the far end of it and far above lies the white mass of Boom Glacier, cradled among the peaks. You can just see, too, streaks in the woods below Boom Mountain; this is the road from Eisenhower Junction through Vermilion Pass to Kootenay National Park.

To Stop 56 — 2.1 kilometres (1.3 miles)

56 Johnston Canyon Stop

Johnston Creek rises in a valley that lies behind the mass of Mount Eisenhower and its subsidiary ridges. After flowing parallel to the Bow River valley for more than 16 kilometres, it turns abruptly south-westward across the trend of the mountains to empty into the Bow River a little below the highway here. Where it cuts across the trend of the mountain ridges it drops through several canyons and water-falls that provide many beautiful views. A short walk up the creek from the parking lot along an easy footpath takes you to some of the nearer of these features. More or less opposite this stop Copper Mountain raises its slabby peak above lower wooded slopes and, to its left (south), Pilot Mountain shows its distinctive snow-covered, sloping head.

Persons travelling north from here can watch the skyline straight ahead for the great brown towers of Mount Eisenhower. Those going south should watch for the spikes and *V*'s of the Sawback Range to the east. An interesting side trip is indi-cated by a sign that points to a walk-ing trail to Lizard Lake, a peculiarly twisted lake marking an old channel of the Bow River.

To Stop 57—5.1 kilometres (3.2 miles)

57 Roadside Stop Near Mount Ball and Mount Ishbel Signs at Beginning of Big Open Meadow

This stop is unusual in that it pro-vides a view of Mount Ball through a gap between Copper Mountain on the right and Pilot Mountain on the left across the Bow River valley. To the east, the jagged outlines of the Sawback Range dominate the skyline. Mount Ishbel is the high peak farthest to the left in the view. You may note the chevron-shaped rock surfaces made by erosion along bedding planes and intersecting joint faces in the massive limestones of the Sawbacks. It is interesting to note, too, how the trees follow the outcropping layers of rocks to make parallel stripes along the mountain slopes because of the different growing conditions that different rock layers provide.

From the southern end of this open stretch you can see the towers of Mount Eisenhower, 13 kilometres or so to the northwest. To its right you can see some of the snowfields that lie at the back of Mount Eisenhower and above a hid-den lake (Rockbound Lake), seldom seen, but a great beauty spot. To the right of that again, Helena Ridge shows a westward dip in its rocks.

To Stop 58—4.2 kilometres (2.6 miles)

58 Alluvial Fan Stop

The road crosses an alluvial fan that issues from a gulch in the Sawback Range, and you can see clearly in several places along the road how a great flush of flood waters has filled

In this unusual canyon in Johnston Creek, about halfway between the lower falls and the upper falls, most of the water tumbles over the edge of a massive rock layer but some squirts out through a hole that the water itself has dissolved.

the woods with limestone boulders and gravelly material. In some places highway maintenance men have tried to control the waters by directing the channels. The general mass of boulders and gravel is referred to as an *alluvial fan* because, as these materials are flushed out of the steep-walled valley behind, they tend to take up a fan or delta shape when seen from above.

*To Stop 59—3.2 kilometres
(2.0 miles)*

59 Stop Beside Muleshoe Lake Picnic Grounds and Plaque

High above this spot the slabby limestones of the Sawback Range are marked in one spot with the Hole in the Wall. This appears to be an old drainage channel, perhaps representing the meltwater from a glacier that was higher up on the mountainside. In some lights the slabby Palaeozoic limestones, here standing very steeply on edge, are very beautiful indeed, with the grey dip slopes contrasting with the shadows and patterns of erosion channels and joints.

To the northwest across the Bow River valley, Pilot Mountain presents its distinctive layer-cake top, and you can easily understand why it was used as a landmark by the pioneers passing through the Bow River valley. From here, too, you can see how the Sawback Range is continued to the south in the Sundance Range, with the Bow River swinging its valley from southeastward to east-northeast across the mountain ridge itself.

A magnificent example of a *hanging valley* is to be seen in the distance across the Bow River valley on a tributary of Wolverine Creek. A tall white ribbon of falling water marks the sheer cliffside, coming from a *cirque*-like valley behind it. Below, on the valley flat, the Bow River has a very serpentine winding course. When the bends of the river become extremely sharp it is not uncommon for some of them to be cut off and left behind on the flat plain. Immediately below the picnic ground, such a meandering loop of the Bow River was cut off naturally and then divided again by the embankment of the railway to form a horseshoe lake.

*To junction with Trans-Canada Highway (Stop 28)—
5.6 kilometres (3.5 miles)*

Roadlog IX
Banff-Jasper Highway from Lake Louise Junction to Bow Pass and Peyto Viewpoint

(Junction of Banff-Jasper and Trans-Canada highways is Stop 45, page 147.)

Junction of Banff-Jasper and Trans-Canada highways to Stop 60—3.0 kilometres (1.9 miles)

60   Stop Beside Herbert Lake

Ahead, or generally northward along the road, you can see the peaks of the Waputik Range across the valley of the upper Bow River. As you swing your gaze to the left, you may note that Mount Bosworth is the last peak before the valley of Kicking Horse Pass, in which lie the main Trans-Canada Highway and the main line of the Canadian Pacific Railway. Left of that again, the first and most distant mountains are the jagged Cathedral Crags in Yoho National Park. Next left, the horizontally layered mass of Narao Peak stands above a dark rock wall stained with dark streaks of water. Mount Niblock with deep *cirques* and horizontal snow lines is the highest near peak and lies at the back of the great rock mass. Still farther to the left is a series of peaks with glaciers here and there. The one in very plain view, with old ice pushing out from underneath last winter's snow, is on Mount Aberdeen, a peak 3,157 metres (10,350 feet) above sea level that lies south of and beyond Lake Louise and the valley behind it. The bulk of Mount Temple raises itself into the southern sky and shows a glacier coming toward you and ending in a great cliff.

The rocks in all these peaks are of Precambrian age in the lower parts and Cambrian in the upper wall, which swings around on both sides to end in wooded spurs, the left one being Mount St. Piran.

To Stop 61—5.0 kilometres (3.1 miles)

61   Roadside Stop

Across the valley, the peaks of the Waputik Range extend northward. Back along the valley and far to the south is Mount Temple's mass, with a glacier on the north side above the great cliff. This is a landmark for many kilometres in the upper Bow River valley. To the right, the white glacier on top of Mount Aberdeen is among the peaks just to the south of the Lake Louise valley. Next is a bowl-shaped cut and Mount Niblock, a horizontally layered knob that stands above a series of ridges and hollows that point to it. Glaciers cover the top of Popes Peak beyond Niblock and a little to the right.

Through the saddle in the skyline made by the valley leading to Yoho National Park through Kicking Horse Pass, the spectacularly glaciered Cathedral Mountain and Cathedral Crags can be seen from here and various places southward along the road for the next kilometre. Northbound travellers should watch for Mount Hector's irregular top, showing horizontal layering in it high above the right or eastern side of the road. Southbound, you should look to the right for a glimpse of Mount Stephen. Far ahead, the jagged top of Dolomite Peak is just visible, framed in the woods on the two sides of the road.

To Stop 62 — 3.2 kilometres
(2.0 miles)

62   Stop at Small Brook

Northward, Bow Peak stands out from the rest of the mountains in a position more or less astride the valley followed by the Bow River. The river and the highway both go out of their way around this peculiar plug in the valley.

Across the valley of the Bow River, the Waputik Range shows the upturned edges of westerly dipping reddish brown quartzites of Precambrian and Lower Cambrian age. You may notice the numerous *cirques* or bowllike depressions in various stages of development and, here and there, white threads of water tumbling down the dark cliffs. These cirques were cut by small local glaciers at a time when the climate was a little cooler than now. Mount Daly lies on the Continental Divide—here the boundary between Yoho National Park and Banff National Park—and just pokes its layered icy head above the Waputik skyline. On its western slopes Daly Glacier covers an extensive area and its meltwaters form several creeks, one of which leaps over the cliffs to form the spectacular Takakkaw Falls in Yoho National Park.

Mount Hector's layered head is seen to the right or east. Far to the south, Mount Temple still shows its large bulk with the glacier on this (north) side. To the right, Popes Peak, with glaciers and patches of snow, is next. On fine days you can just see the tip of Mount Victoria, completely covered in snow and ice, poking up over Niblock's dark shoulder to the left of Popes Peak.

To Stop 63 — 5.9 kilometres
(3.7 miles)

63   Hector Lake Viewpoint

From the eastern shoulder of the valley of the upper Bow River, there spreads below a wide vista of dark forests leading to the bare mountains beyond, providing a lovely setting for the beautiful green waters of Hector Lake. The southern end of Hector Lake lies out on the open

Above: Ptarmigan Lake and Pika Peak are seen here from Fossil Mountain, looking southwestward toward Lake Louise junction. *Below:* This view is from a nunatak, or rock island, in the middle of a very large glacier just west of Mount Drummond, some fifteen kilometres northeast of Lake Louise junction.

Snow Creek wanders back and forth on this sloping valley flat, cutting into glacial debris. It is seen here from near Snow Creek Pass.

valley floor, but the northwestern end heads back into the mountains, with Bow Peak on the north (right) side and the northwestern end of the Waputik Range on the south. This part of Hector Lake marks the place where a large glacier once cut, as you can see from the sheer glaciated walls along the southwestern (left) side. At its upper end, meltwater from Balfour Glacier is bringing down a rush of sand, gravel, and silt, and building a considerable delta.

In the Waputik Mountains opposite, you may note the wall of grey Cambrian limestone overlying the older Cambrian and Precambrian quartzites. All along the edge, *cirques* or bowllike depressions carved by small glaciers may be seen scarring the face of the mountain. Right opposite or perhaps a little to the left, a larger cirque is seen to have a high back wall, patches of dirty snow and *scree* slopes showing in the lower bit with a wooded forelip and small falls visible just below. Here and there, green meadows show where the snow has lain very deep in the winter or where snowslides have cleared out the larger darker trees.

Far to the south through the treetops is the white peak of Mount Temple. Looking northward along the highway and a little to the left, you will see Bow Peak standing out prominently. Although it is really more or less detached, it looks from here to be part of the Waputik Range. It is made entirely of Cambrian quartzite. To the right of Bow Peak you can see the jagged brown outline of Dolomite Peak with other mountains to the right. If you think about the way the rocks dip or slope in all these peaks opposite you and to the north, you will see the key to the larger rock structures in the area. Right opposite, the rocks dip to the west away from you. This you can see especially well at the upper end of Hector Lake. In Bow Peak the rocks are nearly flat, while in Dolomite Peak they dip to the right or east. The combined structure therefore takes the form of an eroded *anticline* or upfold. Still farther right, dips reverse again to the left, showing the position of the next *syncline* or downfold.

To Stop 64 — 7.4 kilometres (4.6 miles)

64 Mosquito Creek Campground Road

Bow Peak presents a wall of pink, brown, and orange quartzite just opposite. Cliffs form where the rock is dense and massive, while more gentle slopes appear where the rocks are more shaly. *Scree* slopes are very common along the foot of the cliffs. Far to the south, Mount Temple's icy top is still a landmark, with its steep sides and its position as the first mountain you see to the right of the Bow Valley. Another glacier-covered peak, Mount Aberdeen, is partly visible through the trees to the right. Below it lies the valley enclosing Lake Louise. Ahead, along the road, a variety of peaks with westward (left) dips line the depression in which Bow Lake lies. Along the east side of the valley, brownish mountains are clearly different from those on the opposite or western side of the valley. This is because they are cut in rocks that are younger than the rocks of the Waputik Range and those in Bow Peak. The distribution of the old and young rocks here is explained on the basis of the regional structure. Bow Peak lies directly on the crest of an upfold or *anticline*. To the west the rocks dip or slope westward and to the east the rocks dip eastward. Rocks in the mountains on

165

the east side of the upper Bow River valley generally dip toward the east in the nearest stretches, but back a little farther you may note that the dip seems to change to a westerly one.

What you are looking at then is a group of rocks that are folded into a gentle *syncline* or downfold and in-cludes rocks much younger than those far below, which come to the surface on the crest of the adjacent *anticline* or upfold as seen in Bow Peak. The very sharp peak to the left as you look south is Mount Hector. It is interesting to note that just beyond the brown rock crests on the east side of the valley, large glaciers and snowfields cover the eastern slopes.

To Stop 65 — 8.2 kilometres (5.1 miles)

This view southeastward from the southern spur of Bow Peak takes in the long western slope of Mount Hector.

Left: Mount Balfour supports a great snow field that feeds Balfour Glacier, whose meltwaters spew a great quantity of debris into the upper end of Hector Lake and form the delta seen in the right of this picture.

Below: The Banff-Jasper highway, seen winding along the valley, sweeps in a big curve around Bow Peak some thirty kilometres north of Lake Louise. Mount Hector, at 3,394 metres (11,135 feet) is at right, with two unnamed peaks nearby.

65 Roadside Stop at Plaque and Outcrop of Dark Green Rock

The only known *igneous* rock—rock that at one time was molten—in Banff National Park is this small body of *diorite* freshly exposed in the road-cut. You can see that it is very dark, and that it breaks out in angular blocks. It has a strong smell of clay when you breathe on it, a sign that it has been altered somewhat. Small patches of a kind of asbestos occur on some of the joint faces and in pockets here and there. It seems to be a tabular mass or *dyke* that has been squeezed into the surrounding rocks at a time when it was molten.

To Stop 66—1.0 kilometre (0.6 mile)

Above: Late evening shadows and highlights make beautiful patterns on the castellated towers and flanks of Dolomite Peak. This peak rises to a height of 2,996 metres (9,828 feet) above sea level.

Opposite: The only known outcrop of igneous rock—rock that at one time was molten—to be found in Banff National Park is this exposure of diabese in a road-cut about a kilometre south of the southern Bow Lake viewpoint. The splash of white just below the centre of the picture is made by asbestos fibres which have spilled from the little ledge just above.

66 Viewpoint, South End of Bow Lake

Crowfoot Glacier sends two long fingers and a short stubby one (with the meltwater stream) over the rock surface opposite this viewpoint from a snowfield that is largely hidden behind the large cliffs to the south or left as you look at it from here. The whole shape of Crowfoot Glacier is much better seen from beyond the north end of Bow Lake because from there you can look into the snowfield itself. The *moraines* below this stop show where the ice used to flow and fall over the cliff, become reconstituted, and then push the debris out from the cliff face itself. At some times of year the contact between the glacial ice, sometimes dirty grey or clear pale blue, and the clean white snow from the past winter is very sharply marked.

Directly opposite, another small local glacier shows dirty ice with white slopes of last year's snow above its rounded and layered tongue. Below it there is a large *scree* slope where the waste from the glacier above has fallen during the year. Some steep declivities are full of last year's snow, and below each of them there is usually a fan of scree or rock waste. Several of these, including the large one below the glacier, are tracked by streaks of fresh debris moved by slides from above and gushes of spring melt-

water. In one place the fresh debris reaches the lake where it is building a delta.

Almost all the rocks in this area are quartzites of Lower Cambrian age that have a general pinkish or brownish tinge, with later Cambrian grey limestones in the higher peaks such as the one beyond Crowfoot Glacier. Southward, Bow Peak stands up in a pointed mass that contrasts in shape with the "long look" seen in the mountains on both sides of the Bow valley; there you can see the edges of rock formations that dip gently away from you on each side. To the left of Bow Peak, Mount Hector stands high and shows some of its very large north- and northeast-facing glaciers. Southeastward down the road, the southeast-sloping masses are Cambrian limestones lying in the *syncline* that parallels, just to the east, the *anticline* along which the Bow River valley is irregularly located.

To Stop 67—2.6 kilometres (1.6 miles)

67 Turnoff at Upper End of Bow Lake

As you stand here and look toward Bow Glacier, your back is to a series of ridges developed in reddish pink and brown Cambrian quartzites that dip generally eastward. You are facing across Bow Lake to the other side of the great *anticline* or upfold

Crowfoot Glacier ends in these long arms draped over the cliffs near the southeastern end of Bow Lake.

where the same Cambrian quartzites dip gently westward. Bow Lake itself presents a beautiful view, particularly when it is calm and the snow-capped peaks, the great cliffs, and the curving *scree* slopes below them are reflected in the calm glacial water.

Across and up the northern arm of the lake, you can see part of a very large snowfield that covers the area of the Continental Divide here for many square kilometres. At this point it sends one icy tongue—Bow Glacier—over the cliffs, showing a rather spectacular icefall before it disappears behind the intervening lip of rock. Behind the lip lies a small meltwater lake whose outlet tumbles over the cliffs and ledges to form the curtain of white water visible from the highway. Below this again the meltwater brook is bringing down a mass of glacial debris to

171

The snowfield above Bow Glacier blends into the clouds in this springtime view over frozen Bow Lake.

build a considerable delta into the west arm of Bow Lake. Portal Peak to the right of Bow Glacier has irregular patches of ice and snow scattered along its bulk.

Southward along the length of Bow Lake, Cambrian quartzites topped by limestone produce an enormous amount of rock debris that has gathered at the foot of the cliffs in superb *scree* slopes. Beyond the south end of the lake and above it, you can see the snowfield and most of the body of Crowfoot Glacier. From the viewpoint to the south end of Bow Lake, very little of the glacier is actually visible beyond the three tongues that spread tentaclelike over the cliffs. To the south, Bow Peak is visible in the gap of the valley and shows the horizontal layering in its Cambrian quartzites at about the middle of the upfold or *anticline* in Bow River

Left: The glacial ice of Bow Glacier can be seen here appearing from underneath the previous winter's snow. This spectacularly crevassed and broken mass is moving slowly down and towards the right.

Below: Magnificent talus slopes, with accumulations of snow, mantle the lower parts of the cliffs around Bow Lake. By mid-June, the spring sun has melted the ice along the shores but has left some in the middle of the lake.

valley. The nearer mountains, particularly under Crowfoot snowfield, on the other hand, show rocks that dip clearly to the west. Left of Bow Peak is the ice-covered top of Mount Hector (see photograph on page 166). When you are nearer to it or on the road to Yoho National Park, you do not see this glacial cap because it is on the back of the peak.

To Stop 68 — 5.0 kilometres (3.1 miles)

68 Bow Summit and Turnoff to Peyto Lookout

Bow Pass, at an elevation of 2,070 metres (6,787 feet) above sea level, is the highest point on the road between Banff and Jasper. You can tell here that you are well up into the mountains for you are much closer to the alpine meadows and the tree line. The air here is generally a little cooler and often has the high-altitude crispness about it.

You are standing at the very beginning of the Bow River, where rain and water from melting snow soak into the ground to come out a little lower down as tiny rivulets that come together to form a gradually increasing stream that enters Bow Lake from the north. Several other brooks, including the ones from the melting of Bow Glacier and those off the surrounding mountains, come into Bow Lake and add their waters to it so that the outlet of Bow Lake is larger than any of the

streams above. As the river flows southward along the valley, gathering contributions from small brooks and the meltwaters of glaciers, it gradually gains volume. It is an interesting river in that all the tributaries that come in from the western side have their headwaters on the Continental Divide itself, either in small streams or in the numerous glaciers along the summits.

To the south beyond Bow Lake, Crowfoot Glacier and the snowfield above it gleam white on the side of the westward-dipping mountains there. A little to the left, the isolated mass of Bow Peak sticks up, interrupting the straight line of the valley itself. Nearer, the ridges on both the left and the right sides of the valley are pockmarked with *cirques,* the depressions carved by small remnantal glaciers. To the north from Bow Summit, you can see along the valley of the Mistaya River for many kilometres with various mountain peaks in the distance. On the left of the valley, one of the landmarks is Mount Chephren's steep-fronted sharp peak with the nearly horizontal snow lines on it, looking rather like a sharp-pointed pyramid.

To Stop 69 — 1.3 kilometres (0.8 mile)

69 Peyto Lookout Area

One of the most beautiful views in the Rockies is from the point of land

a few hundred metres down the trail from the parking lot, for here, surrounded by the mountains, is Peyto Lake, a body of water of incredible colour. Across the lake the sloping Cambrian rocks in Mistaya Mountain provide steep slopes with rock runnels that lead right down to the water. Up the valley (south-south-westward) glimpses of the glaciers leading into Peyto Lake valley and on the Continental Divide nearby show the source of the water here. You can see the greyer fresh rock surfaces recently uncovered by recession of Peyto Glacier. To the right of Mistaya Mountain, parts of the multi-peaked Mount Patterson show beyond the first break. The rocks dip clearly to the west.

The Red Deer River is seen here from a spur of Mount McConnell.

A view northward shows lines of peaks on each side of the valley, those on the east showing eastward dips and those on the west showing westward (left) dips. Thus, the valley is cut into a great *anticline* or upfold of rocks. The brownish slopes to the east are in Cambrian quartzites with greyer limestones above.

The colour of Peyto Lake is very changeable according to the season. Before heavy melting begins, as the winter wanes and summer approaches, the water is more or less a normal dark blue lake colour. However, when the glaciers begin to

The interior country east of Bow Pass features many jagged mountains and small lakes in flat-bottomed valleys.

melt and the water from them picks up very finely ground rock debris, cloudy water begins to come into the upper end of Peyto Lake. As the particle-laden water rushes down and across the conspicuous delta at the head of the lake, the fine particles are kept in suspension. When the water slows to a stop at the head of the lake, the coarser heavier frag-ments settle gently to the bottom, leaving only very finely divided rock flour suspended. This is what gives the lake its colour, and, depending on the time of year, the colour changes as the proportion of suspended material changes. On some days in summer this process presents a spectacular view as the muddy waters coming into the head of Peyto Lake at the edge of the delta make smoky plumes and gradually sink from view into the clear green water.

Above: The part of Bow Glacier that tumbles over the rock wall to the right can be seen from the highway at Bow Lake. *Below:* Peyto Lake, which varies in colour according to the seasons, is seen here looking north. At the left looms Mount Patterson with a height of 3,197 metres (10,490 feet).

Right: From this viewpoint above Peyto Lake near Bow Pass, the end of the spur from Mistaya Mountain shows this great cross section of rocks of Lower Palaeozoic and Precambrian age, dipping or sloping gently towards the west.

Below: The melting waters of Peyto Glacier give rise to this fast-flowing stream, which rushes its load of sand, gravel and silt to the south end of Peyto Lake. Here it has built this delta, which is gradually filling in the lake basin.

Roadlog X
Banff-Jasper Highway from Bow Pass to North Saskatchewan River Crossing

Peyto lookout and junction at Bow Summit to Peyto Glacier viewpoint—2.7 kilometres (1.7 miles)

70 Peyto Glacier Viewpoint

Peyto Glacier appears as a long tongue of dirty ice poking down the headwall of the valley below the fresher-looking snowfields above. Below it and on the sides you can see bare rock that used to be covered with ice a very short time ago, but which has been laid bare by the shrinkage of the glacier itself. Another glacier may be glimpsed to the right of Peyto Peak opposite, with a deep *V*-shaped stream valley coming out from it. Two small hanging glaciers on the wall opposite and to the right lie in *cirques* on the flanks of Mount Patterson. The left one has a thread of meltwater and a perfect fan far below. The right one spills over the rock wall and is reconstituted below the summer waterfall and at the top of a very long rubbly slope. Along the line of peaks to the right, the sharp head of Mount Chephren stands out and is a landmark up and down the valley for many kilometres. To the east, or behind you as you face Peyto Glacier, the slopes are made of quartzite and limestone of Cambrian age.

To Stop 71—4.5 kilometres (2.8 miles)

71 Mount Patterson Viewpoint

A most unusual set of masses of glacier ice with several arms and isolated bits is hung over the wall of Mount Patterson directly opposite. On calm days in summer the roar of meltwater streams is constant. On the wooded lower slopes, scars of rock and ice slides through the dark trees show as bright green where small bushes and grass grow. To the right of the glaciers, one very brown rock runnel is visible in the Cambrian quartzites in the lower slopes. Well below the present ice masses, twin *lateral moraines* make an unusual sharp-crested horseshoe, clearly delineating that the many bits and arms of the glacier above were once part of a larger glacier that occupied the whole of the steep-backed glacier bowl or *cirque*. Southward, the white of Crowfoot snowfield and glacier is visible high up and to the right.

Northward, along the highway toward Jasper, Mount Chephren shows its very distinctive peak, with a steep front but not quite so steep back. Its shape and marked horizontal layering make a landmark that is

Remnants of a once much larger glacier are draped over the rugged rocks of Mount Patterson's northeast slope.

visible for many kilometres on either side. On its south side, snow-filled gullies in late summer make a giant *H* in white against its dark rock flanks. Behind and to the east are the brown Cambrian rock slopes of Mount Weed.

To Stop 72 — 3.8 kilometres (2.4 miles)

72 Crossing of Silverhorn Creek

As you face westward across the valley (to the left if you are going north) a whole array of jagged limestone peaks is in view. Ebon Peak is the farthest back and the highest, standing some 2,928 metres (9,600 feet) above sea level. Glaciers are to be seen here and there among the peaks, including pieces of fairly large ones, which lie along the Continental Divide south (left) of Ebon Peak. The bulk of Mount Patterson dominates the scene directly to the south. Its lower slopes lead into a valley that is obscured from here by the low intervening wooded ridge. This valley houses Mistaya Lake, another beautiful pale green to turquoise jewel like Peyto Lake a little to the south. From Bow Pass northward, water begins to collect from small rivulets into small brooks which unite their waters and gradually in-

180

crease the volume of the thread of water, lower down to become the Mistaya River. This river gathers its headwaters from Peyto Glacier and others along the Continental Divide, as well as a contribution from the mountains on the east side, to flow, some 40 kilometres farther downstream, into the North Saskatchewan River close to the highway crossing.

The nearer peak to the right is grey Cambrian limestone clearly dipping away from you. The nearer ridge is in the Lower Cambrian orange quartzite, whose colour is most clearly shown in the numerous rock runnels and slides. The mountains ahead and to the left seem generally to be brown and thinly layered, and to consist of rocks that lie above the quartzite group. For the most part they are horizontal, or dip gently to the right or east as you look northward toward Jasper along the highway.

To Stop 73 — 0.6 kilometre (0.4 mile)

73 Barbette Glacier Viewpoint

What is unusual from here is a view, nearly south, up into the valley where the lower part of Barbette Glacier fills a very large bowl or *cirque* depression in the mountains. It is dazzling clean white on top, with the dirty older ice oozing out from beneath its lower edge. The ice is full of rock debris and dust near its foot. Although not visible from here, the bottom of the valley you are looking into is occupied by Mistaya Lake, about 3 kilometres long and of the same very beautiful pale green and turquoise colour of many of the lakes into which fresh glacier meltwater discharges.

Barbette Mountain rears its snowy head some 3,074 metres (10,080 feet) above sea level, back of and to the left of the glacier. Mount Chephren's front spike and higher back peak are about at right angles to the right from Barbette Glacier. Beyond the reddish Lower Cambrian quartzite hill to the left of Chephren, Howse Peak is a jagged mass of pale buff dolomite above a wall of grey limestone.

On calm days here the distant roar of meltwater can be heard in the mountains.

To Stop 74 — 3.7 kilometres (2.3 miles)

74 Upper Waterfowl Lake and Howse Peak Viewpoint

Along the highway in this section you are on the northeast side of the Mistaya River and various lakes that lie in its course. Looking westward and southwestward across the valley, you can see high mountains that lie on the Continental Divide to the left and others that lie a little north of a westward swing in the Continental Divide to the right.

Spectacular glaciers are found to the west-southwest of the Waterfowl Lakes. This is Conway Glacier, and the dark stripe is its medial moraine.

Chief among the latter is Mount Chephren, the great rounded point of rocks that is conspicuously layered, with dips inclined very gently toward the west. The lower part is made of quartzites of Lower Cambrian age, and you will notice their reddish or pinkish cast on *scree* slopes and places where the rocks are broken. Higher up in the peak, the quartzites give way to grey limestone that extends all the way to the tip. You can see a back peak a little to the left or west, made entirely of the grey limestones that slope gently westward, consistent with those in the tip of Chephren itself. Mount Chephren is a landmark because of its height of 3,268 metres (10,715 feet), its distinctive shape, and its position as a projection from the west wall of the main valley system that the Banff-Jasper highway follows.

To the left of Chephren, Howse Peak at 3,294 metres (10,800 feet) rears a jagged head of pale buff dolomite above grey limestone walls that continue to the left along the spectacular skyline. Mount Patterson thrusts outward beyond a major glacier-headed valley and shows patches of ice and snow on its front (east) face. Away to the south, the white patch is Crowfoot snowfield, south of Bow Lake, seen close up from Stop No. 66. The rocks of these mountains are Cambrian

Opposite: Freshfield Glacier, one of the most spectacular in the Rockies, lies some fifteen kilometres west of the Waterfowl Lakes.

quartzites in the lower orange-red slopes, younger Cambrian limestones farther up, and some Ordovician limestone and dolomite in the tips of Chephren and Howse Peak.

To the east, the peaks are ribbed horizontally and generally have a brown colour. Some, particularly those that are back a bit from the road, have lower slopes in the brownish Lower Cambrian quartzites but extend well up into the Middle Cambrian and Upper Cambrian limestones. One set of peaks beyond a conspicuous side valley shows grey limestone cliffs in the lower reaches, a much-ribbed shale sequence, and their peaks just barely extending into an upper limestone sequence with sharp spires and towers formed in it. To the northwest you can see again a line of peaks (Kaufmann Peaks and perhaps a little of Mount Sarbach) mostly made of Middle and Upper Cambrian rocks and, in the very tops, rocks of Ordovician age.

To Waterfowl Campground road— 1.9 kilometres (1.2 miles)

One of the foot trails from this campground leads (a walk of about an hour and a half) to Chephren Lake, a beautiful pale green body of water that extends in a valley right to the foot of Howse Peak. Another trail from here goes to Cirque Lake, a little bit to the south, also extend-

ing right into the foot of the very high mountains. At each place you can see the grey Middle and Upper Cambrian rocks almost down to the bottom of the mountain with the reddish Lower Cambrian quartzites in the very lowest slopes, glaciers hanging on the mountainsides, and numerous *moraines* showing where they once spread.

To Stop 75—0.6 kilometre (0.4 mile)

75   Lower Waterfowl Lake Viewpoint

If you look up the lake and beyond to the south, you will see Mount Weed on the left with its rock layers dipping eastward (left), and Mount Patterson and other peaks directly opposite it across the valley with a westward (right) dip. This shows clearly that that part of the valley with the highway and the river lies just about squarely on the crest of an upfold or *anticline*. You should therefore find the oldest rocks exposed in the centre of the valley and, sure enough, that is where Lower Cambrian pinkish and reddish quartzites are found, with younger Cambrian rocks forming the flanks of the mountains on either side; still younger rocks occur in the tops of the mountains on both sides of the valley, some of Ordovician age. Where you are standing, on the other hand, you find that the road and valley have swung east-

ward off the main axis of the anticline so that the rocks in the adjacent peaks clearly dip eastward and those on the mountains opposite, such as Mount Chephren, are nearly flat on the eastern slopes, swinging gradually over toward westerly dips farther back.

Directly opposite, over the wooded slopes, is Howse Peak with glaciers on its right (as you look at it), in the saddle and on ledges. It is largely made of grey and buff limestones of Middle and Upper

Chephren Lake lies in a deep bowl below Mount Chephren, Howse Peak, and the flanks of Mount Synge.

Cambrian age and may even include some Ordovician rocks at its peak. The Kaufmann Peaks to the right of Chephren are generally the same. All along in the lower hills you will notice the reddish Lower Cambrian quartzites sticking out. Here and there to the east (back of you), massive limestone cliffs are of Upper Cambrian and even Ordovician

age because this area is on the eastern flank of the anticline and the rocks are dipping to the east; as a result of this, the farther up or the farther east you go, the younger the rocks will be.

Away in the distance, a large white patch of snow straight down the road to the south is Crowfoot Glacier and snowfield. Directly opposite again, you might notice the two small glaciers on Chephren's lower flank. The left one has last year's snow and dirty ice below, with a conspicuous *terminal moraine* ridge below it. The other is largely covered with snow and has big pull-away cracks where the snow has settled down toward the terminal moraine below it. Both come from the accumulation of snow falling from above and they are good examples of glaciers that are formed far below the real snow line of the area. Grassy green slopes covered with low bushes to the right, below the peak, mark where slides of rock and snow have cleaned out the trees. Chephren Lake lies in the valley beyond the ridge across the lake. It is another of the beautiful green to turquoise scenic gems

---

Opposite: Mount Chephren thrusts its horizontally layered head to 3,266 metres (10,715 feet) above sea level. In this late June view, the Mistaya River, seen here in the foreground, reflects the highlights from the woods and mountains.

found in the Rockies below the glaciers and may be reached by a foot trail from the Waterfowl Lakes campground just south of this stop.

To Stop 76 — 6.7 kilometres (4.2 miles)

76 Roadside Viewpoint

High above you to the east lie the enormous grey and yellow cliffs of Mount Murchison, a huge mass of Cambrian and Ordovician rocks on the eastern flank of the great upfold or *anticline* along which the valleys of the Mistaya River and the Bow River, far to the south, are located. Northward along the highway the mass of east-dipping limestone of Mount Wilson stands out prominently with some of its very large snowfield showing as a white topping along its crest and back. In a *V*-valley about halfway along the width of Mount Wilson, a white line is made by an unusual stream. Keep an eye on it, for when you are closer you will see that it has no head. The rocks in Mount Murchison and Mount Wilson are generally Upper Cambrian in the very lowest slopes, with a great thickness of massive limestone and alternating limestone and shales forming the cliffs from the timber line nearly to the crest. The uppermost cliffs, you may note as you look into the gullies, are very light coloured. These are made of the Ordovician Mount Wilson

187

quartzite, a strongly cemented sandstone.

Opposite this viewpoint the long line of the Kaufmann Peaks exhibits Middle and Upper Cambrian limestones, with some Ordovician rocks in the top parts. Glaciers in various forms and shapes occur here and there along the higher parts. Mount Chephren's distinctive tower, with reddish quartzites and white snow fans near its bottom, gives way to the westward to a higher limestone peak with two lovely white glaciers on the top, both ending in great break-off cliffs of dazzling white ice.

To Stop 77—5.6 kilometres (3.5 miles)

77 Roadside Stop at Middle of Long Hill Opposite Restraining Fence

Behind and up the hill, the great limestone walls of the Kaufmann Peaks end to the right in Mount Sarbach, with several lovely glaciers hanging on the upper slopes. Mount Sarbach is the *type locality* for some of the Ordovician rocks of Banff National Park, with its lower slopes in Upper Cambrian rocks. Across the valley of the North Saskatchewan River, which, on joining with the Howse River swings abruptly to the northeast from its prevailing south-easterly course, you will see the great bulge of Mount Wilson. You can see stripes of green vegetation parallel to the rock formations alter-

nating with great grey cliffs. This is because the rock units are different from layer to layer; the massive limestones break off to form the cliffs, and the softer, more shaly layers weather more rapidly to form chip-covered scree slopes, which in some places allow vegetation to take hold. The rocks there dip east on the east side of the anticlinal structure that the main valleys of the North Saskatchewan and Mistaya rivers follow. A little farther down the hill along the highway, you can see exposed in the cut-through flanks of Mount Wilson the synclinal structure to the east, with a conspicuous valley occupied by Owen Creek just about on its axis.

High above you to the southeast, the towers and cliffs of Mount Murchison reach toward its summit some 3,335 metres (10,936 feet) above sea level. To the northwest, straight left as you face downhill along the road, the group of high mountains includes Survey Peak on the left and, way beyond it to the right, Mount Amery with the horizontally layered, flat, plateau-like top. Dark limestones in the road-cuts are of Cambrian age.

To Stop 78—1.1 kilometres (0.7 mile)

78 Turnoff and Signs for Various Trails, Including Mistaya Canyon

The Mistaya River, gathering its waters from the glaciers along the

188

Left: The Mistaya River plunges into a deep gorge a few kilometres south of where the Banff-Jasper highway crosses the North Saskatchewan River. The rounding in the walls of the canyon is typical of gorges cut in limestone.

Below: Mount Chephren, seen here across Lower Waterfowl Lake, is cut into flat-lying rocks of Lower Palaeozoic age. The pile of gravel and boulders to the left of centre is a small terminal moraine.

Right: Mount Wilson shows its rugged western face in the late afternoon sun. A large snowfield covers the mountain just behind the very sharp edge on the top. The valley extending to the left is that of the North Saskatchewan River.

Below: Another view of Mount Wilson, seen here from the Adventure Road, shows very clearly how the alternating layers of east-dipping limestones and more shaly rocks give the mountain a banded appearance.

Continental Divide and the streams that flow off the mountains in the east side of the valley, drains all the valley followed by the Banff-Jasper highway from the North Saskatchewan River crossing back to Bow Pass. A few minutes walk from this viewpoint will take you down through deep woods along a well-marked path to the river itself at a point where it leaves an open flat-bottomed valley and plunges into a deep, vertical-walled, very narrow canyon. Beautiful *potholes* in all stages of development—made by the solution of the limestone and the wearing away by boulders being whirled about in the currents—mark the area. Below the bridge, the grey limestone rocks line the walls of a canyon that is typical of many of the mountain-stream valleys in Banff National Park—very deep, with the rumbling water far below still cutting, abrading, and dissolving the rocks wherever it can.

To Stop 79—3.7 kilometres
(2.3 miles)

79 North Saskatchewan River Crossing

From either end of the bridge over the North Saskatchewan River you can see two kinds of water in the river: grey silty water of the North Saskatchewan on the north side, and green clear water from the Mistaya River on the south. In sum-mer the distinct colours persist to well below the bridge before mixing obliterates them.

From the bridge, from the first kilometre or so of the Adventure Road, and from the Warden Station south of the bridge, an unusual brook can be seen on the south-facing flank of Mount Wilson. A very white ribbon of rushing water makes a conspicuous mark on the darker rocks of one of the gullies to the right of the main peaks. As you follow it upward you may note that it suddenly stops. If you were to climb up there, you would see that it gushes as a full-fledged stream out of an opening in the rocks to cascade on down the surface of the moun-tain. It must have its origin in the melting ice and snow on the back of Mount Wilson's summit, then plunge into underground solution channels to pop out at the surface here.

Roadlog XI
North Saskatchewan River Crossing to Sunwapta Pass

North Saskatchewan River
crossing to Stop 79a —
1.0 kilometre (0.6 mile)

79a Viewpoint at the Top of the Hill, to the Left

If you walk out through the skirt of trees to the point of land where the picnic table is, you can enjoy a superb view.

Here, you are near the right-angle change of direction of the North Saskatchewan River, from the southeasterly course it follows for many kilometres to a northeasterly one. The Howse River carries an equal volume of water into the elbow of the North Saskatchewan River from the southwest. Just below the viewpoint you can see where the combined waters of the two streams flow in numerous channels separated by islands of sand and silt deposited by the river waters themselves. You also become aware of the two great mountain masses marking the ends of the great ridge of mountains that parallels the Banff-Jasper highway on its eastern side for many kilometres. On the northern side of the elbow is Mount Wilson, 3,242 metres (10,631 feet) above sea level at its summit and covered with a great snow- and icefield on its back or northeast slope. On the southeast side of the North Saskatchewan River gap is Mount Murchison, even higher at its summit at 3,333 metres (10,930 feet) above sea level, but with only small patches of ice on the back or eastern slope. Both these mountain masses represent enormous piles of Cambrian sedimentary rocks at their bases and Ordovician sedimentary rocks through most of their exposed, cliffed, upper parts. From the parking place, two of the farther back (and right) peaks of Mount Wilson show topmost cliffs in grey to white Mount Wilson quartzite, of Ordovician age.

Below you, the braided North Saskatchewan River shows numerous sand and gravel terraces on its sides. To the left as you face off this viewpoint (southwesterly up the valley of the Mistaya River), Mount Chephren rears its steep-fronted tower with two very white glaciers on its high back peak (right). Straight westward, a major fork in the river valley shows the Howse River coming in from the left and the Glacier River in the valley to the right. The mass of mountains in the fork of the rivers is culminated in two sharp peaks, the nearer being Mount Outram at 3,254 metres (10,670 feet), and Mount Forbes at 3,630 metres (11,902 feet), the farther and sharper. At one time the travel route westward up the North Saskatchewan River and following beyond the elbow along the Howse River and through Howse pass into the valley of the Blaeberry River, was very seriously considered for the main transcontinental railway and road system. To the right as you look out from the viewpoint, great masses of nearly horizontal brownish rocks extend from Survey Peak on the left to the high flat-topped and steeply cliffed Mount Amery on the right. From the parking place, the edges of the snowfield to the left of Mount Amery hang over vertical walls of rock more than a thousand metres high.

The structure of the mountains to the east of the main North Saskatchewan - Mistaya River valley is clearly a *syncline* or downfold in which the rocks dip toward the centre from both sides. You can see this from various points on the highway in this general region by looking southward toward Mount Murchison or northward toward Mount Wilson. This is an astonishingly persistent rock structure, for it is the same syncline that you can see between Mount Eisenhower and Helena Ridge nearly 130 kilometres to the south, and it extends northward to within sight of Jasper, some 130 kilometres to the northwest. In some places the long stretches of the road and the main river valley lie in the upfold or *anticline,* while in others they wander a little bit eastward off the anticlinal axis into the synclinal structure itself.

Viewpoint to junction with David Thompson Highway to east— 0.5 kilometre (0.3 mile)

Whether you are travelling north or south, it is worth a short side trip east along the David Thompson Highway. About 0.5 kilometre (0.3 mile) down the road, a view up the slopes of Mount Wilson shows clearly the headless stream high on the mountain. In late summer when all the other gullies dry up, this one is still full of rushing white water, for it comes from melting snow and ice on the back of Mount Wilson and reaches the head of the apparent part through underground passages. Another 5.6 kilometres (3.5 miles) along the road is the crossing of Owen Creek. To the westward, back along the road more or less, are the two guardian ramparts of this part of the Saskatchewan River valley. To the left or south is Mount Murchison with its east-sloping rocks that continue on into the peaks behind it, then flatten to horizontal in the middle of the syncline, and then reverse to westerly dips in the mountain to the left of that. Right up the valley to the north, the same syncline is visi-

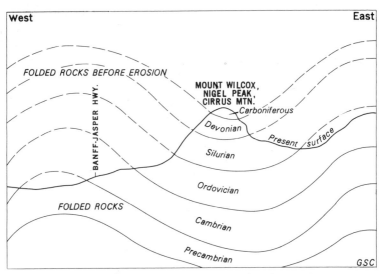

Region at north end of Banff National Park, looking north.

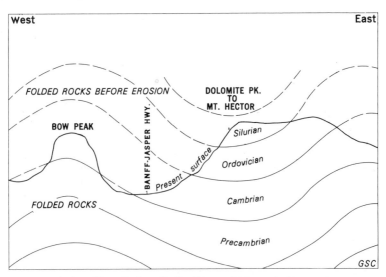

Region of Bow Peak on the Banff-Jasper Highway, looking north.

ble again with far peaks showing horizontal caps. Some of the ice on the back of Mount Wilson is also visible.

Away beyond the park boundary to the east, younger more shaly rocks compose the hills, and slopes are more slack and gentle.

*Junction with David Thompson Highway to Stop 80 —
6.4 kilometres (4.0 miles)*

80   Roadside Stop on Long Straight Stretch

As you look south along the highway, Mount Murchison's huge mass of Cambrian and Ordovician rocks dips gently to the left or east. A little to the right of this, Chephren's tower peeks out from behind the foreslopes of the jagged-topped Mount Sarbach with a long, vertically ribbed wall of grey limestone. Mount Sarbach is the *type area* for the Sarbach Formation of Ordovician age. Cambrian rocks extend all along the fronts of the mountains to the north or right. The nearer peaks of the great mass to the north are not named, but the northern arm of the great horseshoe is Mount Amery. On the nearer sides of this complex, two great *cirques* or bowls with vertical walls, lined with *talus* along their backs, lie below the snow to the right and the great ice cliff on the left. The left cirque is much deeper, probably the result of

greater erosion because more snow fell into it from above. A third, smaller cirque is just under the peak to the right, making a bowl-shaped depression with a canyon cut recently by the meltwater stream coming from it. Mount Hooge opposite, with a castellated and jagged top behind and above the near flanks, shows once again snow lines leading down into glacial bowls—one in front of the nearest peak just above the skyline and the other behind that but in front of the great rock-walled, higher peak. Survey Peak rises to the left of these above an old forest-fire area. To the east, the great rugged cliffs of Ordovician rocks along the face of Mount Wilson form the backing to the highway. Towers of white Mount Wilson quartzite of Ordovician age are visible in the very tips of the peaks.

To Stop 81 — 3.2 kilometres (2.0 miles)

81   Roadside Stop Below Waterfalls

It is worth stopping here a moment to look at the waterfalls high in the great limestone cliffs on the western slope of Mount Wilson, just east of and high above the highway. On most days the wind playfully blows the water aside so that it lands in different places at different times, wetting a considerable area. In late

The towering bulk of Mount Murchison, cut in Cambrian and Ordovician rocks, stands above the valley of the North Saskatchewan River. Note the well-marked timber line and the steepness of the cliffs.

summer it may dry up altogether. However, in times of heavy melting of the snows above, the waters gush down the gullies and wash down a lot of rock waste, thus accounting for the fan of rock debris that the road crosses just here. You may note large and small boulders of dense white quartzite in the debris in the fan. These come from the Mount Wilson quartzite (Ordovician age) forming those dark-stained, white-to-buff cliffs in the highest peaks and towers on both sides of the waterfall creek valley. Some of the bouldery gravel from this deposit has been used in construction of the road.

In the cliffs to the north, the rocks all dip toward the east, contrasting with those in the mountains across the valley westward where they are generally horizontal. This means that here you are on the east-dipping side of the anticline that you have been following for so long.

To Stop 82 — 1.1 kilometres (0.7 mile)

82 Roadside Stop in Long Straight Stretch of Road

Across the valley to the west, you can see an outstanding example of what snowslides do when they come crashing off the crests of the ridges to go avalanching down the valley side, clearing out the trees and carrying them far below. You can see places that have been cleaned bare with rock runnels going down them, and other places that have been stripped of the dark woods and now have only light green grass or low bushes growing. Wooded ridges are protected on their upper ends from the avalanching snow by projecting rocks, and you can see many variations of these. On some of the ridges, where the snow is shed sharply to either side, the trees reach all the way to the top, while on the gentler ones the snow has cleared quite a lot of the ridges themselves.

To Stop 83 — 1.9 kilometres (1.2 miles)

83 Rampart Creek (Stop Just North of Culvert)

Westward, you look up the valley of the Alexandra River, its heavily wooded lower slopes leading upward to the rocky peaks. Mount Saskatchewan is on the north or right side as you look at it from here and encloses a huge glacial bowl in horizontally layered rocks, with a couple of tall *needles* to the right of the main peak. On the south side of the Alexandra River valley, Mount Amery rears its horizontally layered, flat-topped, cliffed summit. This mountain lies at about the axis or crest of the *anticline* or upfold that the road follows along, and just east of, for tens of kilometres. For this reason the rocks in it, being of Cambrian age, are older than those on either side and are flat-lying. On Mount Amery's flank a very deep valley cuts into the brownish and greyish (upper) slopes, making a horseshoe-shaped ring of mountains. Far to the south down the valley, Mount Chephren's tower peeks from around Mount Sarbach's rugged and snow-patched top. The glorious white gush of Rampart Creek comes from melting glaciers on the back or east side of the mountain here. All along the eastern part of the valley the grey cliffs continue, but it is interesting to note that the rocks are not all the same age in these cliffs, for the fold structures all the way from Bow Pass to Sunwapta Pass gradually *plunge* northward. This means that younger and younger rocks will be seen the farther north you go. Here, the

Unseen, except by the most adventurous, this meltwater lake lies east of the great line of cliffs in the upper valley of North Saskatchewan River, about opposite Cirrus Mountain campground.

lower parts of the cliff are in Ordovician rocks while the upper parts are in Devonian rocks.

Persons going north from here may look into Mount Amery's great horseshoe *cirque* and see the magnificent rim of ice—actually cliffs of ice that are many tens of metres high—on the top of the cirque wall.

To Stop 84 — 5.1 kilometres (3.2 miles)

84 Roadside Stop Beside North Saskatchewan River, at South End of Long Straight Stretch of Road

The view here, almost from river level, shows a wide flat of sand and gravel carried here by the North Saskatchewan River from the northwest and by the Alexandra River from the west. You can see how the sediment-laden water is cutting in some places, filling in others, and spreading its load of rock waste out over the valley floor. From the deep grey colour of the water, you can just imagine how much sediment must be carried past this spot every year.

The mountains, from which the waste is coming, surround you on all sides. To the right of the Alexandra River valley are the brownish slopes of the lower spurs of Mount Saskatchewan and, beyond it, the horizontally layered top with the patches of snow. These contrast with the dark, heavily wooded, lower slopes in the valley of the Alexandra River itself. South of the Alexandra River valley, Mount Amery raises its flat-topped head with the great snow- and icefield at the very top. A large *cirque* or bowllike depression carved by a remnantal glacier lies on the front of Mount Amery as you see it from here.

The rocks in both Mount Saskatchewan and Mount Amery lie almost exactly on the crest of the upfold or *anticline* that parallels the valley of the North Saskatchewan River. That is why the rocks there are horizontal whereas those back of you (east) dip to the eastward and, out of sight from here, those to the west of these mountains dip generally to the west. This also accounts for the fact that the flat-lying Cambrian strata of Mount Amery are complemented on both sides by younger rocks, which dip off the anticlinal structure. The brown-weathering shaly and limy rocks of the spur of Mount Saskatchewan opposite are of Upper Cambrian age and show the eastward dip of the east limb of the anticline, contrasting with the horizontal layers of Mount Saskatchewan on the axis of the fold a little to the west.

On the left side of the valley looking south are the tremendous grey limestone cliffs of Mount Wilson, with walls and spikes of the grey and white Mount Wilson quartzite at the very top. Beyond, in the distance, the same kinds of rocks make similar cliffs on the front slopes of Mount Murchison.

To the south of the front peak of Mount Amery, you can look into the great horseshoe *cirque* on its east side with its rim of dazzling white ice.

To Stop 85 — 5.3 kilometres (3.3 miles)

Overleaf: The North Saskatchewan River, seen here looking northwest toward its junction with the Alexandra River, wanders in slow graceful curves through a wide gravel-filled valley bottom. In the background, the great limestone mass of Mount Saskatchewan can be seen with its peak almost invisible in the glare of the setting sun. This towering limestone mountain, with its distinctive peak, rises to 3,342 metres (10,964 feet).

85 Roadside Stop Beside North Saskatchewan River, Opposite Rock Ridge in River Bottom

The North Saskatchewan River, loaded with silt, sand, and gravel, is interrupted in its free flow here by a ridge of rock that you can see very clearly in the river bottom. The river has cut through at two different places but now is only using the lower one, and it pours its whole mass of grey silt-laden waters through a narrow gap in the rock wall. Opposite, the wooded hillsides show great sweeping scars made by snowslides in late winter and spring. The trunks of trees from the darker forest are left as tangled masses at the foot of the hill, with quick-growing low bushes and grasses marking the snowslides with a trail of contrasting light green. The brown waste-covered slopes you see here and there across the valley to the west are in Cambrian shale and limy shale. Away to the south, the tip of Mount Chephren with its white glacial top is framed in the river valley. To the right, a little bit of the ragged top of Mount Sarbach, some 30 kilometres away, is just visible.

Across the valley and diagonally to the right, Mount Amery raises its grey horizontally-lined walls of Cambrian limestone, capped by a dazzling white mass of ice and snow. All along the east side of the valley the limestone cliffs gradually increase in height as you travel northward and, right here, are made of Ordovician and Devonian rocks.

To Cirrus Mountain campground — 4.2 kilometres (2.6 miles)

Cirrus Mountain campground to Stop 86 — 0.6 kilometre (0.4 mile)

86 Viewpoint, Under Limestone Cliff and Beside River

The awesome cliffs of grey limestone to the east of the highway here make you feel pretty small. The falls at the campground in summer are only small shadows of their size during the spring when melting snow all over the upper mountain slopes pours water into the brooks coming over the edge. As you look at the cliffs, you may notice that rocks in the top part show a north-easterly dip, much more gentle than the steeply dipping layers on the other side of the valley and in two of the brown peaks far ahead. Once again this is because of the position of the valley on the major fold structures. To your back and out of view is Cirrus Mountain, which lies more

---

Opposite: The view from the brown ridge, which separates the valley of the North Saskatchewan from that of the Alexandra River, shows the latter's beautiful braided channel. Beyond are the east-dipping rocks of Mount Wilson and, in the distance, the flattening dips in Mount Murchison.

Above: Mount Saskatchewan is seen here from the brown ridge. *Below:* This view of its jagged towers can be seen from several places along the Banff-Jasper highway between the junction of the Alexandra and North Saskatchewan rivers and the Cirrus Mountain campground.

or less in the centre of a downfold or *syncline* so that the rocks in its peak are much younger than the cliffs you are looking at nearby, and are nearly flat-lying. The sign points to it, but from here you can see only the lower half. Stop No. 88 provides a view of the whole mountain. The rocks in the cliff right behind you dip underneath the mountain as do the more steeply dipping ones on the other side of the valley. Still farther to the west, beyond the steeply dipping rock beds, the layers are flat-lying again because they are on the crest of the next anticline. As you look generally down the river valley, the brown Upper Cambrian shaly limestone subsidiary ridge from Mount Saskatchewan sticks out into the main valley. Beyond that, the horizontal layer cake of Mount Amery, with its Cambrian limestones, shows the lovely white frosting of the icefield on its very top.

To Stop 87 — 1.8 kilometres (1.1 miles)

87   Weeping Wall Viewpoint
Several little creeks come over the edge of the enormous cliff of grey Devonian limestone and fall more than one hundred metres in a series of sheer falls, interrupted by ledges along which water flows a short distance and then tumbles over again. Southward, Mount Amery raises its

castellate top with lines of snow and ice, displaying very clearly the horizontal bedding and its icecap on top, with sheer cliffs several metres high along the edges. Northward is Parker Ridge, with the scar of the road on its right or eastern side, showing the sweeping lines of the west limb of the syncline with its easterly and flat dips. One could judge from this that as you travel northward the road gradually moves closer to the axis or the trough of the downfold or syncline. Nigel Peak, to the right, shows part of the axis of the syncline, although the preponderance of westerly dips shows that much of the peak lies just east of the fold axis. Note the steep easterly dips in the wall of limestone directly opposite (west of) this stop.

To Stop 88 — 4.3 kilometres (2.7 miles)

88   Viewpoint Overlooking Valley on Curve Opposite Gravel Bank
Those travelling north along the Banff-Jasper highway have noted that between the Weeping Wall viewpoint and this one the road has climbed more than a hundred feet and just here has swung westward more or less across the trend of the valley, so that you can look a long way down it. The magnificent cliffs of Devonian limestone in the bottom of Cirrus Mountain to the left

Right: The snowy peak of Mount Saskatchewan lies above a massive wall of limestone. Snow cascades from the steep upper slopes to form the pile at the base of the cliff. As it gradually pulls away from the cliff, it leaves the *bergschrund*—the great cracks that can be seen near the summit.

Below: Here, to the north of its junction with the Alexandra River, the North Saskatchewan River cuts directly across the edges of an upturned rock layer.

contrast with the soft smooth slopes made by the brownish Banff shale above it and the cliffs of grey Rundle limestone in the peaks. Here is the same formational rock sandwich, Palliser-Banff-Rundle, that is seen in so many of the spectacular mountains in the southern part of Banff National Park, where the road leads through the Front Ranges of the Rocky Mountains. Mount Rundle and Cascade Mountain were two superlative examples of this scenic rock sandwich, you may remember.

The brook in the foreground comes from the glaciers on the north slopes of Mount Saskatchewan and rushes down its steep course to join the North Saskatchewan River. Beyond are the peaks of Cirrus Mountain.

Looking back to the Weeping Wall, you can see how the falling waters originate in the melting snows, then flow into and under the *talus* slopes and through the woods to emerge and then plunge over the great cliffs.

Saskatchewan Glacier is one of several tongues of ice that come off the great Columbia Icefield in the region where Banff, Jasper and Hamber parks meet. This view from the top of a ridge can be reached by a footpath from the main highway.

The synclinal arrangement of the rocks is very clear from this viewpoint, with the change in dip from westerly in the left part of the view to easterly at the cliffs on the east side of the river valley. Slabby dip slopes of limestone and shaly limestone opposite give way below to great talus slopes with big boulders and fine debris mixed, making very beautiful patterns of shadows and light when the sun is at the right angle.

Here and there to the west from this viewpoint are peaks and patches of ice. One especially glorious, white, broken glacier is on the south side of Mount Athabasca to the right of the major valley. Although out of sight from here, this valley is occupied by a very

large tongue of ice, the Saskatchewan Glacier, which gathers its substance from the Columbia Icefield, a unique mass of glacial ice and snow that covers many tens of square kilometres along the Continental Divide. At that place on the Continental Divide, the precipitation in the form of ice and snow is shed in three different directions: via Saskatchewan Glacier and the North Saskatchewan River eastward to Hudson Bay; northward in several places including Athabasca

This boisterous meltwater stream comes from the glaciers on the north side of Mount Saskatchewan.

Glacier into the Sunwapta River, the Athabasca River, and ultimately the Mackenzie river system to the Arctic Ocean; and southwestward through Hamber Provincial Park (B.C.) to join the Columbia river system and the Pacific Ocean. A spurt of water on the left side of the Saskatchewan Glacier valley indicates a *hanging valley* there.

The rocks beside the bridge which spans the gorge of Nigel Creek, to the north end of the park, are Middle Palaeozoic limestones, layered almost horizontally.

Southwest from here in the woods, you may note a wild boisterous waterfall over bedrock and boulders, where a tributary to the North Saskatchewan River comes in from the mountains to the south. On days when it is hot in the snowy mountains, melting supplies a lot of water. It is indeed a wild and beautiful sight with the water bouncing and tossing over and among the boulders and rocky ledges on its way to join the North Saskatchewan River below. You can see where this brook joins the North Saskatchewan River on the flat below at the foot of the right and smaller of the two *scree* fans. You

---

Opposite: After crossing the flat of gravel below Parker Hill, this brook plunges into a deep canyon near the road to reappear a kilometre away, far below.

210

might note on the valley flat, away below and to the left, the much clearer waters of Nigel Creek as they appear here and there in turns in the wooded flat. Close to the fence, you can look below and see the deep limestone gorge cut by the North Saskatchewan River. It is as little as one and a half metres wide, but it is more than 30 metres deep in some places. Along the curve of Parker Ridge the road has made a vast cut in glacially deposited gravels in the upper slopes, and talus slopes in the lower ones.

To Stop 89 — 0.8 kilometre (0.5 mile)

89 Roadside Stop at Junction of Old Road

The old Banff-Jasper highway used to branch off the present route, cross the North Saskatchewan River here, and swing tightly down around the wooded hills to the right as you face downhill. This spot is a very interesting one because at and just below the old highway bridge the muddy waters of the North Saskatchewan leave the flat, open, gravel-strewn valley bottom to plunge into an extremely narrow and very deep limestone canyon, in places only a few centimetres wide. It is visible here, and again on the old highway where a second bridge crosses it. At this lower locality, the very deep narrow canyon echoes the rumble of the waters of the North

Saskatchewan several metres below, mostly invisible because of the crooked and curved walls of the canyon itself. Another feature of the old road is its nearness to a set of wild waterfalls, which are utterly spectacular when great torrents of meltwater in summer pour off the mountains. These were the falls mentioned at Stop No. 88. The walk down the old road to these places is indeed an interesting and exciting one.

To Stop 90 — 0.8 kilometre (0.5 mile)

90 Valley Flat Viewpoint

The main Banff-Jasper highway makes a sweeping curve over the spew plain of the North Saskatchewan River. You can see how the river's channel has been completely reorganized to allow the highway to be placed where it is on the gravel plains. The river has been directed to one side and put into a straight channel, with great quantities of the gravel formerly on the valley flat now used to build the roadway itself. For a time during the rebuilding of the highway in 1961-62, a very large construction camp occupied the middle of this grand circle.

One of the most unusual features to be seen from this stop is the wild waterfalls on the south side of the North Saskatchewan River. In summer, meltwater from high up in the mountains comes tumbling down as a fairly rough brook for several kilometres. Then it spills down a steep-walled chute and at a certain level is flung out in intermittent jets, which fall into the valley below.

Westward across the gravelly flats, you can see where the North Saskatchewan River comes out of a little gorge in the rocks. Above this gorge a very extensive gravel flat lies below the foot of Saskatchewan Glacier, where the river begins in the melting ice.

Parker Ridge, with a light grey lens or wedge of *reef limestone* in the cliffs, lies ahead. To the left in the woods, outcrops of Mount Wilson quartzite are visible and accessible. Brownish slopes of Cambrian limestone and shaly limestone appear to the west.

To Stop 91 — 1.4 kilometres (0.9 mile)

91 Viewpoint Halfway up Parker Ridge

A superlative view of the syncline in Cirrus Mountain is offered from this spectacular viewpoint. The valley of the North Saskatchewan River leads southward into the distance. Far below, it passes under the great cliffs of Devonian limestones with the Alexo Formation and Fairholme Group in the lowermost slopes, and the major part of the very steep upper cliffs in the Palliser limestone. The upper slope of the Palliser limestone forms the clearly shown shoulder, above which lies the more gently weathering brownish Banff shale, of Mississippian age. The top peaks of the mountain are again in grey limestone — the Mississippian Rundle limestone. As you swing your gaze from side to side in this mountain, you will see that the rocks on the right or southwestern end of the mountain dip generally eastward while those on the other end dip generally westward, and the troughlike synclinal arrangement is clear.

From this viewpoint you can look down and see the new highway below and parts of the old highway to the west of it, with glimpses of various streams on the valley bottom. The clear water of Nigel Creek contrasts with the much muddier silt-laden water of the North Saskatchewan to the right. Directly opposite, on the western side of the valley, enormous dip slopes of grey limestone have vast fans of debris below with great boulders and chunks of limestone showing on the surface.

This viewpoint also allows a look southwestward up a considerable valley to the snowfields in the distance on the northern slopes of Mount Saskatchewan. It is from this ice- and snowfield that the water comes to produce the boisterous waterfalls mentioned at Stop No. 88.

Steeply dipping limestones, lit by the late afternoon sun, make this spectacular view, seen from the curve of the road at Parker Hill. The talus slope has come from a rock slide just above its apex.

(These falls are just visible down the hill on the road.)

A scene of great beauty lies to the east where a tributary of Nigel Creek falls more than one hundred metres to form Bridal Veil Falls.

To Stop 92 — 0.5 kilometre (0.3 mile)

92 Upper Parker Ridge Viewpoint (Panther Falls)

Those travelling north may, at this viewpoint, review some of the sights seen from the lower viewpoint, half a kilometre down the hill. Two very spectacular waterfalls make the stop here worthwhile. Across the steep limestone valley a

Opposite: A small brook tumbles in graceful falls over the edge of the canyon of Nigel Creek. It is seen here from the lookout at the top of Parker Ridge.

tributary to Nigel Creek drops over in a slender cascade called Panther Falls. A walk over the bank will take you to the lip of Panther Falls, where the main body of water of Nigel Creek plunges over the limestone cliffs into the canyon of its own cutting far below. When the wind is right, you can feel the cool spray as it blows up from the falls.

To Stop 93 — 2.9 kilometres (1.8 miles)

93 Nigel Peak Viewpoint

As you look northward along the main Banff-Jasper highway here, a high knob, Nigel Peak, lies just to the right of centre along the valley, more or less on the centre of the *syncline* or downfold. Westward, dips on its right flank and the peak next to it are clearly visible. As you follow to the left, you can see the dips flatten and change to the east. A southerly *plunge* is visible in it, so that the rock structure resembles a canoe with one end higher than the other. The low left flank of the hills shows clearly its eastward dip. Across the road to the west, the steeper eastward dip of limestone layers visibly flattens near the crest.

This beautiful example of a cirque, or glacial bowl, is carved into the limestones of the mountain slopes near the northern end of Banff National Park to the east of the highway.

216

The fold in Nigel Peak is the same downfold or synclinal structure visible in Cirrus Mountain to the south and is, in fact, the same syncline seen off and on along the Banff-Jasper highway all the way south to the Mount Eisenhower area. The corresponding upfold or *anticline* lies to the west, and the east-dipping slope of Parker Ridge can be considered to be either the west limb of the syncline or the east limb of the anticline. Nigel Peak itself has the Rundle limestone on top with the brownish Banff shale in the intermediate slopes and the grey cliffs below forming a wall along the valley in the Palliser (Devonian) limestone. The same synclinal structure extends northward for many kilometres too, and is visible at several places along the Banff-Jasper highway in Jasper National Park, ending in the synclinal Mount Kerkeslin within sight of Jasper itself.

Across to the east, the valley of Nigel Creek swings generally eastward toward Nigel Pass and marks the boundary between Banff and Jasper parks. This valley forms the principal means of access to the Brazeau River country and the southeastern corner of Jasper National Park. From here you get a glimpse deep into the back country.

Banks of snow are to be seen along this stretch of the highway during most of the year. If you look at the surface of the snow patches, you will almost invariably find that it has a dimpled pattern.

To Stop 94 — 2.1 kilometres (1.3 miles)

94   Stop at End of Parker Ridge Trail to Saskatchewan Glacier Viewpoint

This section of the Banff-Jasper highway winds along the valley between the ridge made by Nigel Peak and its subsidiary spurs on the east, and Mount Athabasca and its spurs on the west. From some spots along here, Mount Athabasca is a partial matterhorn spike left by the carving of bowl-shaped *cirques* by glaciers on its flanks. One of these cirques, with a glacier in the bottom, lies right below the peak and to the left.

The trail to the top of Parker Ridge follows up the dip slopes of limestone rock beds in Parker Ridge itself, switching back and forth all the way to the top. From the top is a breath-taking view out over the valley of the North Saskatchewan River, taking in the mighty Saskatchewan Glacier, with its great

---

Opposite: This beautiful icefall is on the southern shoulder of Mount Athabasca and high on the northern wall of Saskatchewan Glacier. In the foreground, the bouldery debris carried by other glaciers that once occupied the large bowl contrasts with the limestone cliffs seen in the background.

dark *medial moraine* coming from the Columbia Icefield to the west.

The walk to the top of the ridge is well worth while, for at the top you have the feeling of being a real mountaineer, in the wilds at an elevation of over 1,800 metres and with a superlative view in many directions.

To Stop 95 — 4.3 kilometres
(2.7 miles)

95 Banff-Jasper Boundary and Cairn

The Banff-Jasper highway in the next few kilometres to the southern Jasper boundary passes along a valley filled with large quantities of glacial sands and gravels. Road-building operations have interfered with many of the natural exposures, but stream banks still show a few. At this high elevation trees grow only in a few sheltered places, and true alpine meadows are common in the valley bottom and on the flanks of the hills.

Along the east side of the valley is Nigel Ridge leading to Nigel Peak. This mountain mass is directly in the axial part of the main syncline, that is, in the bottom of a canoe-

Mount Athabasca is the tall peak just right of centre, with the mass of glacial ice below it. This mountain is one of the highest in Banff National Park, rising to 3,491 metres (11,452 feet) above sea level.

221

This cairn, constructed of rocks of the Spray River Formation, marks the boundary between Banff and Jasper parks. It also marks the divide between waters that flow southeast to end in Hudson Bay and those that flow northward to the Arctic Ocean.

shaped downfold. Erosion has removed both of the limbs, so now you see only the centre part of the syncline with the rock beds dipping in on each side. As you look along the slopes, you may notice a dark band across the spurs about halfway up. This may possibly be the Exshaw Formation, a puzzling dark formation of questionable age that is known very widely in the Banff-Jasper area. It separates the Banff Formation above it and the Palliser Formation below, seen here in the lower cliffs. The uppermost few metres into the peak area belong to the Rundle Formation, so here we are again with the Palliser-Banff-Rundle formational rock sandwich seen in so many major peaks in southernmost Jasper National Park and in Banff National Park. The Fairholme Group underlies the *talus* slopes at the base of the mountain as seen from here.

Open meadows in the uplands areas are the true *alps*. Notice as you look at the hillsides that trees grow in sheltered spots where they are protected from the wind and crushing accumulations or slides of snow. The upper limit of trees or the *timber line* is highly variable, depending as it does on protection, soil, drainage, and a lot of other things.

As you stand here at the cairn on the boundary between Jasper and Banff national parks, you are on the divide from which the waters split to flow northward into the Sunwapta river system and ultimately via the Mackenzie river system to the Arctic Ocean, and southward into the North Saskatchewan River and finally Hudson Bay. From the posi-

tion of the cairn and the boundary where it crosses the highway, it is somewhat difficult to visualize how water would flow into one valley and the other because the road here is angling along the side of the hill; but when you look at how the water actually flows, you can see that this is indeed the divide.

Looking northward from the boundary into Jasper National Park you will realize that these beautiful mountains extend for hundreds of kilometres. The great rock structures stretch uninterrupted into Jasper Park, for the pass at the boundary is only an accident of erosion. The mighty synclinal fold, seen here and there for so many kilometres along the road in Banff National Park can be seen ahead in Jasper National Park beyond Nigel Ridge. The high mountains along the left extend on into more beautiful mountains, culminating, in this view, in the ice-covered crest of Mount Kitchener. The back slopes of Columbia Icefield show here and there among the mountains.

For those travelling northward toward Jasper, it may be noted that the guidebook to Jasper National Park—*Behind the Mountains and Glaciers*—has a roadlog, like this one, that takes you all through Jasper National Park. Stop No. 1 in the Jasper book is the same as this stop in Banff National Park.

This mysterious water,
Substance of our own being,
Melding of all the rains that have passed this way
And some that issued from among the stones of springs,
After dark, mysterious journeyings in subterranean channels
And echoing in unsighted caverns
Now sparkling especially brightly.

David Baird

Epilogue

Deep within all of us there is something that is stirred by the beauty of our natural environment. Tall rocky peaks, mirrored in the calm green waters of a mountain lake, may move us to reflective thought. The roar of a waterfall and the tingling of spray on our faces, or the distant boom of falling ice in the glaciers may intensify the sense of beauty already richly felt from what we see. A knowledge of what we are seeing and of what is happening now in the long procession of natural events can only increase the awe that is felt amid the magnificent surroundings in Banff National Park.

Rows of parallel mountains that alternate with open valleys result from millions of years of erosion in complicated and massive rocks, twisted and folded and thrust up thousands of metres by enormous stresses inside the earth's outer framework. Ancient rocks that once were soft muds stirring to the wash of waves in the bottom of shallow warm seas now ring the bowl-shaped depressions filled with ice and snow on the mountain peaks. The paths where families now walk along wooded mountainsides or above the timber line may once have been the shoreline of a shallow sea. Tents are set up and evening meals prepared where mighty glaciers once thrust their icy tongues and, in their long drawn-out melting, spewed out immense quantities of sand and gravel in their meltwaters to floor the valleys with the waste of the mountains nearby.

All around, you can see how nature is seeking to redress imbalance created usually by some other adjustments of things out of balance. Stresses deep within the earth cause great faults or breaks and one part of the surface is uplifted. Rivers and glaciers promptly start wearing away the uplifted land. A river changes course slightly and wears away against a different bank. Rocks, at one time muds, then hardened under pressure, now slowly weather away again to form new mud. Sandstone and conglomerate, once sand and gravel on shores and ancient stream beds, return again to sand and gravel. These processes have gone on for millions of years before we arrived on the scene, and that little bit of them we can see in our lifetime will form but a tiny part of an even longer story.

Thus, when you see a tiny drop of water ooze out of the moss, gather body, then fall to the wet ground below, you can think that it is beginning a long trip to the sea, perhaps 5,000 kilometres away, and forming, too, a tiny part of the systems of rivers and streams that are gradually wearing away the land. When you see a snowflake fall in the late autumn or winter, you can think that it may be five hundred years before those beautiful crystals of ice finally emerge from the foot of a glacier as meltwater. When you look into the face of an alpine flower to see its delicate symmetry and to discover a drop of nectar hidden deep in its secret places, you can think that its substance springs from its roots in the soil where thousands of years of weathering and wastage of rocks has gone on before. When you sit beside a rushing stream or a turbid mountain river, you can think that the suspended mud may have taken a thousand years to come from the tops of the wasting peaks, or again that it was formed only yesterday where one boulder fell against another and scraped off some of its substance. When you see the ancient grey limestones in the valley walls and in the peaks of the mountains, you can think that hundreds of millions of individual living creatures lived their brief span and left their shells to accumulate on the sea bottom to help make the rock. When you see the life of now—the trees, the squirrels and bears, the flowers and birds, and even the people—you can think of that vast unfolding story of life that goes back for at least six hundred million years, and wonder about what we are doing here.

Index

For more information on the geology of Banff National Park see the following publications:

A Guide to Geology for Visitors in Canada's National Parks, by D. M. Baird. Published by Macmillan Co. Also available from Publishing Centre, Supply and Services Canada, Ottawa K1A 0S9, or from any of the national parks. This pocket-size book describes the general principles of geology with special references to the national parks of Canada and is written in layman's language (about 160 pages, 50 illustrations).

The Story of the Mountains in Banff National Park, by Helen R. Belyea, Geological Survey of Canada, 70 pp., 37 figs. (1960). A general guide to the geology and scenery of Banff National Park.

Alberta Society of Petroleum Geologists—Guidebook, Fourth Annual Field Conference, Banff-Golden-Radium, 1954. This book includes general articles on the geology of the area, and roadlogs for certain of the highways. Generally a professional approach but contains much of interest to the layman as well. Available from the Alberta Society of Petroleum Geologists, 631 8th Ave. W., Calgary, Alberta.

Geology and Economic Minerals of Canada, Economic Geology Series No. 1 (6th ed.) of the Geological Survey of Canada. This compilation of the geology of all of Canada contains a great deal of information on the western moutains. Available from Publishing Centre, Ottawa, or from the Geological Survey of Canada, Ottawa.

Particular questions of a geological nature concerning Banff National Park should be addressed to the Director, Geological Survey of Canada, Ottawa, or to the office of the Geological Survey in Calgary or Vancouver.

For information on all other matters concerning the park, write to Parks Canada Information Division, Ottawa K1A 0H4.